THE ART OF THINKING

The ART of
THINKING

Chats On Logic

SECOND EDITION

KNOWLEDGE • UNDERSTANDING • WISDOM • TRUTH

SILVANO BORRUSO

DAVID'S PUBLISHING
SCARBOROUGH, ONTARIO, CANADA

THE ART OF THINKING—Chats on Logic

Second Edition

Silvano Borruso

Copyright © 2016

Published by:
David's Publishing
Scarborough, Ontario, Canada
dave1hogg@gmail.com

ISBN: 978-0-9950876-0-6

Cover design and interior layout: Juanita Dix • www.designjd.net

TABLE OF CONTENTS

PREFACE

A handicap of modern education is to assume, without proof and against the tradition of millennia, that the innate ability to think is the same as that of thinking systematically. Give good instruction in a number of appropriately chosen subjects, conventional wisdom says, and thinking will take care of itself.

The experience of the ages says otherwise. For centuries Logic, the craft that taught that art, was obligatory in the Western tradition before university admission.

An account of the demise of the teaching of Logic is beyond the scope of this work. So too is the proper remedy, a manual expounding the rules of systematic thinking.

My aim is more modest, but no less telling. I am no scholar and make neither the pretence of being one, nor of addressing this book to scholars. I write for young adults of school-leaving age and also for mature adults who have never been taught the art of thinking. You who read this, if you judge that schooling and extra-curricular activities have somehow short-changed you, this book is for you. Conversely, if you belong to the world of scholarship and are acquainted with the rules and regulations of Logic, read no further.

I aim at making you aware that there is more in the world than apparently meaningless routine. One of the reasons why the world appears bereft of meaning is that the powers of the mind are usually untrained for a deeper understanding of reality.

Instead of abstractions difficult to remember and inapplicable in real life, here you will find examples of how real thinking and life are inseparable. I have called them "chats" because every chapter is a self-contained unit, not necessarily a logical sequence from the one immediately before it. But I trust that you will find the art of thinking much more enjoyable when exercised in day-to-day occurrences.

At the end of most chapters I have appended a list of characters that appear in text but are perhaps unfamiliar to readers.

INTRODUCTION

Thinking is like a well-constructed building, resting on foundations that support visible structures in a functional order. As in a building, the foundations are invisible but solid, lest the superstructure collapse into rubble. A building has also a certain amount of decoration, not to be confused with the load-bearing framework.

Facts, necessarily multiple and varied, are the raw material of thinking. You have acquired most of them in childhood, in and out of school. You will acquire more as time goes on, some of it, I hope, within the covers of this book. However necessary for thinking systematically, the knowledge of facts is not, strictly speaking, thinking, any more than raw materials: stones, tiles, etc., are the building itself.

Systematic thinking begins with **understanding**, a rarer and more precious commodity than just facts. Your school textbooks have packed your memory with oodles of facts, but seldom have they provided understanding. Unlike the knowledge of facts, understanding is the ability to see connections between one fact and another as between facts and real life. You must have noticed that whenever you have experienced understanding, in or out of school, it has caused a certain joy difficult to describe. In the process, it has also embedded whatever you understood in your memory for good.

Understanding, then, is like a building slowly acquiring its intended shape and function from purposefully assembling its raw components. The experience of understanding powerfully suggests that the knowing process, despite appearing so diverse, is really one, potentially now, actually in the future.

But understanding cannot be taught as knowledge can, no more than a building can be put together by a manufacturer of bricks and tiles. You can cram knowledge into your head, which most probably you did before exams. You must have experienced, though, that crammed matter stays there, if at all, for the duration of whatever exam you sat and disappears soon after.

In this book you will find many examples of understanding, often at surprising day-to-day levels that you never thought could belong together. That is how real life is, and how much more exciting than sense experience understanding is.

Last in systematic thinking comes wisdom, the art of ordering factual knowledge and understanding into an enduring intellectual edifice. A good building shows an ordered use of space, a proportional distribution of masses, no afterthoughts, additions, unnecessary openings, etc., in a word, functionality. It is the same with thinking. Ordering the thinking materials, however, is more difficult than understanding, for it does not pursue just any order. It pursues the order of the universe, the cosmos, striving to reproduce it within the mind.

Accordingly, the book consists of three parts, dedicated to factual knowledge, understanding and wisdom respectively. Some, but not all, of the rules of logic will appear, aiming at arousing enough interest for you to pursue the subject wherever and whenever convenient.

PART ONE

THE RAW MATERIALS: FACTUAL KNOWLEDGE

There are three, and only three, ways of acquiring factual knowledge: by the evidence of the senses, by proof, and by testimony. You trust your eyes telling you at this very moment that you are reading a text: no one has to prove that to you. But if you want to know whether the paper of this page is made from rags or from wood pulp, or whether it is acid free and the like, the evidence of the senses is not enough; you need proof. This you can get from having the paper analyzed in a laboratory.

Neither your senses nor any amount of proof will answer the following: How do you know that I, the author of the book, am truly the person whose name appears on the cover? Or for that matter, how do you know that I, and no one else, wrote the text you are reading? There is no way of knowing all that except by trusting me who affirm both things, in other words by accepting my testimony.

Of the three pathways, the first and third provide factual knowledge. The second (proof) provides digested knowledge, for it requires understanding chemical analysis. This part on raw materials, therefore, is about knowledge attained by sense action and by testimony.

CHAPTER 1

OBSERVATION

Inanimate Things

Wherever there is a functioning eye there is vision, but not necessarily observation. The difference lies in how much attention the mind pays to what the eyes see. You must have seen a soda bottle top hundreds of times and know that its sides are machine-crimped so as to make it grip the bottle hermetically. Now answer the question: "How many crimps does it have?"

If you can answer, it means that at some time, perhaps out of curiosity, you have practised observation by **counting** those crimps. If you cannot, you have not counted them, and it is no use guessing. You **must** count them, and you will never forget it, because all soda bottle tops have the same number: 21.

The example is a trifling one, but it shows the difference between seeing and observing.

A more complex example is a soccer ball, which again you must have seen many times even without playing the game. Even a cursory look will tell you that its spherical surface is tessellated by pentagons and hexagons. Can you tell how many of each?

This time you are observing a sphere, and if you try to count the two sets of polygons by revolving the soccer ball, you will soon become frustrated and give up. Now think again: is there a simpler method of solving the problem?

There is, if you recall that a sphere always shows half its surface. If therefore you hold the soccer ball at arm's length with a pentagon smack in the middle of it, you will easily count 6 pentagons and 10 hexagons. Multiplying by two you get the answer: 12 and 20.

The two examples show two characteristics of observation: first it sharpens the power of the senses; second, there are correct and incorrect methods of observation.

There is more: observation has practical, real life consequences. If you own a sewn article like a wallet or a handbag, after some time you notice that lengths of stitches give way here and there. Before throwing the article away in disgust, pick it up and **observe**. You will notice two threads running on either side of the sewn surface; invariably one of them (the one that does not show) is much weaker than the other. Whereas the morality of making and selling such an article need not concern us, the observation it affords does.

The difference between the two threads is the clue that the article is machine-sewn. If you own a sewing machine, make a point of observing how it works, by hand rotating it slowly while looking at its mechanism below the table. The machine **locks** the stitches against one another by an ingenious mechanism. You can duplicate the lockstitch by hand, but no machine can duplicate the hand-produced double cobbler stitch, a single thread running back over itself either in fabric or in leather.

If you re-sew by hand the machine stitches that have failed, the resulting double cobbler hand stitch will prove a great deal stronger and more durable than the machine's. And you will save money and time both in the short and in the long run.

Living Things

By observing living things you will quickly realize that their elements follow patterns, and that some patterns are all-encompassing.

One of them is the Fibonacci sequence, each element of which is the sum of the previous two: 1, 1, 2, 3, 5, 8, 13, 21, 34, 55, 89, 144 etc. The ratio between any two elements approaches φ, the Golden Ratio 1.618034... Protracted observation uncovers this series, and the ratio: in the arrangement of leaves on stems, of petals on flowers, of joints on bones, of growth curves in shells, and of all kinds of structures distributed in a practical infinity of samples. Entertainment is assured and endless.

People

The foregoing examples have been of things, but another important field of observation is people.

Whether at school or at home or among friends or at work, you must have noticed that some people attract your sympathy, others leave you indifferent, and for still others you feel antipathy. But why should it be so? Can you reasonably account for such attraction-aversion?

There is more. While textbooks have sanctimoniously preached to you "human equality" you could not help observing the opposite. Throughout your experience of life, however long or short, you have met people who are better than you at some endeavours, but worse at others; which means that such people are equal (to you and to each other) as persons, not as the idiosyncratic individuals you have observed. Absolute equality, or identity, is not the hallmark of nature. Not even two leaves of the same tree are identical to one another.

So far, so well observed. Now, can you account for it? Remember, observation is a piece of raw material, be it a foundation stone or a roof tile; it reveals no more than the sheer strength of one of the elements that make up the building. To answer the question, as to explain many other things, requires both understanding and wisdom, to be seen in Parts Two and Three.

The Self

Let us finish this section with the most difficult type of observation: that of the self. If your parents have helped you in the fascinating but never-ending quest for self-knowledge, you may already know a good deal about yourself. You may have become alert to some formerly hidden but now budding abilities and to some avoidable but annoying defects. To the bits of information we acquire from our parents or from other persons we are continually adding insights from our own observation.

For instance, can you recall the first time you disagreed with your parents about something serious, like choosing a school or travelling on your own instead of being driven or chaperoned here and there?

If that is a vivid memory, you are recalling the first time you observed **yourself**. For the first time your thinking was **independent** of that of your parents. You had acquired the awareness of being a **person**. Not that you were necessarily right in your standing, but the very existence of the disagreement was a healthy symptom that your thinking was developing along independent lines.

Now let us be clear about independent thinking. If you disagreed with your parents in order to agree with peer pressure, your thinking was certainly **different** from that of your parents, but in no sense independent. Your thinking was now dependent on that of your age mates, who strongly influenced you.

The foregoing assertion does not give enough information to conclude that independent thinking is always correct whereas dependent thinking is not. There is only one value that makes for correct thinking, independent or not, and it is the **truth** of things. Why?

Truth **is ownerless**: it belongs to all. We possess truth when our mind agrees with things outside it. Therefore, if two people agree on something true, they **remain free from each other**. But they may agree on something false, either proposed by one of the two or by someone whose proposition they both accept. What happens? The proposer of falsehood, present or absent, enslaves those who accept it. They are now bound not to a common reality but to a person who has severed the link between the mind and things.

Please note again that we do not have enough information to conclude that this enslavement is in any way voluntary and therefore evil, or whether it is even understood as such. But enslavement it is, and that is how important **loyalty to truth** is. If you give little or no importance to truth, and lead your life by values that exclude it, do not read further; this book is not for you. But if you value truth above all things, you will come to understand and experience the real meaning of *"the truth shall set you free."*[1]

To illustrate, take **compassion**, the ability to suffer with those who suffer and rejoice with those who rejoice. It is an excellent and praiseworthy virtue, but separated from truth it has invariably undesirable and often downright noxious consequences.

Many equate compassion with giving money to the poor. Nothing wrong with that, but experience shows that doing only that keeps the poor in poverty for good. This is true whether

---

1. Jn 8:31-32

it is the rich who dish out the money, or today, increasingly, the State, or the less poor, etc. The truth is that only human work produces wealth. When people are given enough incentives to work and are allowed to keep the fruits of their labour, they unshackle themselves from poverty and acquire dignified wealth. Here is an example from real life.

On one occasion I ordered a set of school desks from a large woodworking concern owned by Sikhs. On entering the premises, the place looked as if it had suffered a fire not long before. It had, but the place was in full production less than a week after the accident.

It had happened that on hearing of the fire, members of the community had immediately offered to help with **large sums of money**. The owners declined, remarking that before they could undo the damage **months of production** would be lost. They asked instead for the **loan of machines** until they could repair their own, and this was immediately acted upon. Lost production amounted to no more than a couple of days. Money (compassion) would not have solved the problem. Machines (compassion plus truth) solved it.

CHAPTER 2

TESTIMONY

By listening to parents, teachers and friends, and by reading books in and out of school, you have by now an impressive array of factual knowledge. You may add TV watching, even though images are forgotten more easily than the spoken or written word. Most of those facts you have never experienced personally, and in all likelihood you never will, from remote areas described in geography books to experiments described in science textbooks.

Even though internet makes it possible to get more information about places than you could possibly get by actually going there, and show you live experiments performed by experts, you will forever have to accept on trust that characters like Julius Caesar and Alexander the Great have existed. Most of what we know we know on **trust**.

There is a school of thought, among many, maintaining that we know best what we come to know by ourselves. True enough, but as remarked earlier we cannot rely exclusively on self-attained knowledge. Were we to do that, neither would we progress much as individuals, nor would society. Intellectual progress is but the knowledge of previous generations added to one's own, afterwards handing over the package to the next generation. Individual as much as social knowledge is **cumulative**.

Here there is a hitch. How do we know that knowledge received by way of testimony is **true**? The unfortunate answer is that we do not know, for we humans are only too prone both to be in error ourselves and to deceive others.

You are old enough to have been personally present at some event that the media reported next day. Was what they reported what you saw? If the answer is "no", either always or most times, you realize that it is prudent to take the so-called "news" with a large pinch of salt. This is not to say that reporters deliberately deceive us but that they themselves are not always free from error.

Reporters are in good company. Historians, scientists, and other purveyors of information are not above misrepresenting facts. At times they omit vital information; at others they add unnecessary truths or downright falsehood to a true account. As a result, those at the receiving end are prevented from understanding what actually happened, and further judgement is invariably distorted.

The Truth

A way to detect problems of testimony is to compare a description of the same event in two different sources: newspapers, historians or, increasingly, internet. Assessing and analyzing such reports, as we shall do right now, will contribute to forming a rock-hard critical mind.

Textbooks and assorted readings (even internet for that matter) may have convinced you that the ancients believed the Earth to be flat. They are supposed to have persisted in this misconception until Columbus discovered America, or Sir Francis Drake circumnavigated it, or Galileo proved it to be spherical, etc.

The three statements are disinformation. None is true. The first to hold that the Earth is spherical was a Greek called Archelaus', reputed teacher of Socrates, who lived in the 5th century B.C. Aristotle made the common sense observation that only a spherical body could cast a circular shadow on the Moon in an eclipse. In 250 BC Eratosthenes of Cyrene, the librarian of Alexandria, actually measured its circumference, by means of geodesical principles valid to this day. Given the inaccuracy of his measuring instruments, though, he made an error of about 10%.

To those who argue that the reputedly ignorant and backward Middle Ages lost this knowledge, you may recommend the study of astrolabe construction. This instrument was in use for more than 2000 years, and countless samples of them are kept in many museums.[2] To construct an astrolabe, it turns out, one **must** assume the Earth to be spherical, so as to project its southern hemisphere on a flat surface.

---

2. In pre-internet days an excellent article appeared in *Scientific American* January 1974.

Professional historians may not blunder about Galileo's proving the Earth round, but history teachers do: one of them asserted it to me personally. He must have heard it as a schoolboy, never bothering to verify it. The fact is that the Earth had been circumnavigated 42 years before Galileo was born.[3] The sailor was not Sir Francis Drake (1540-1596) as another history textbook must have assured him, but Juan Sebastián Elcano on the *Victoria*, the only surviving ship of Magellan's expedition beyond the Americas and across the Pacific.

School is not the only place where falsehood passes as fact. The surrounding cultural atmosphere, mainly by repetition, tends to instill a *forma mentis*, a way of thinking clashing with reality. For instance, you must have grown up convinced that progress is inevitable. To be "progressive" is a badge of honour of sorts. Once a certain "target" however dubious, is attained, "there is no going back", for the target, whatever it was, "has come to stay".

To dispel that conviction, think of four pieces of "progress" that backpedalled in 1991 in a **little more than a week**: Leningrad reacquired its old name of St Petersburg after 70 years; the German Bundestag (Parliament) returned the capital city to Berlin after 45 years. Slovenia and Croatia became independent for the first time in history; and the Knights of Malta returned to the island[4] whence Napoleon had expelled them 200 years earlier.

---

3. Or earlier if the 1421 Chinese account of the same feat by Admiral Zheng He (1371-1433) is to be credited.
4. As representatives of the Order, not as masters of the island.

A curious example of mental sclerosis is the assertion, endlessly repeated especially in the English speaking world, that 13th century theologians used to dispute on how many angels could dance on the tip of a needle (or of a pin, not much larger).

Arnold Lunn (1888-1974) took them to task in four pages of his 1950 *The Revolt Against Reason*. He quotes Cyril Joad, famous British agnostic of the first half of the 20th century:

In the Middle Ages most people believed, indeed it was an article of faith, that a certain number of angels could dance on the point of a pin, and the great question was as to how many there should be.[5]

Joad had written this in 1941. In the attempt "to track down this rubbish to its source", in his own words, Lunn could go no further back than a 1638 quote by a certain William Chillingworth. The allegation does not appear in any 13th century source, and its being an article of faith is Joad's pure invention, or thoughtless repetition.

One would think that the matter should have been laid to rest in mid-20th century, but it was re-offered 42 years later by no lesser a luminary than Robert B. Reich, former Labour Secretary of the first Clinton Administration:

Such questions (old economic categories) provide endless opportunities for debate, not unlike the argument by thirteenth century Scholastics over how many angels could comfortably fit on a pinhead.[6]

---

5. Eyre & Spottiswoode, p.231-32.
6. *The Work of Nations*, First Vintage Books p. 94

The irony is that he should compare a piece of thinking obsolete by decades with one obsolete by centuries. Internet does not seem to have put a stop to such inane quests.

Distortion of fact is relatively easy to dispose of, unless embedded in a reference work, in which case it becomes practically impossible. But it requires overcoming mental laziness.

The Whole Truth

It is much more difficult to spot omissions (or deliberate suppressions, you never know) of fact, for that requires going to the sources. At least one has to know where to locate them.

The first example comes, amazingly enough, from an actual source, the Bible. A born-again friend, eager to produce a Biblical backing to his assertion that all you need to be saved is to accept Christ as a personal saviour, quoted Acts 16:31-32. The jailer of Paul and Silas asks what to do to be saved. Sure enough, the answer is

Believe in the Lord Jesus and you shall be saved, you and your household.

But the story does not end there. The very next verse 33 says

He and his family were baptized immediately.

How this verse escaped my friend's attention I don't know. But escape it did, and as he stared at me uncomprehendingly,

I recalled a practical joke our teacher played on our raw minds in primary school. He asked: "How many months of the year have 30 days?" When we rattled the conventional answer "four!" he gave us a cold shower pointing out that he had not asked how many months had **only** 30 days, so that the correct answer was "eleven". Only February does not have 30 days.

This story goes to show that when a vital piece of information is either missing or missed, the perspective of the issue changes considerably.

Take the historical event known the world over as the Boston Tea Party. It is a fact that an entire consignment of tea, taxed by the British Government at 3 pence per pound, was thrown into the Boston Harbour in protest against that tax. It was December 16th 1773.

Adding nothing more, one gets the impression that the "patriots" had a legitimate grudge against being taxed without representation at Westminster, so that their leader Samuel Adams was an American hero, immortalized to this day in a popular brand of American beer.

Ezra Pound (1885-1972) has a different story to tell:

The cardinal fact of the American Revolution of 1776 was the suppression, in 1750, of the paper-money issue in Pennsylvania and other colonies, but history as taught in the U.S.A. speaks of more picturesque matters, such as the Boston Tea Party.

In other words the Party is a cover-up for something much more momentous that was going on behind the scenes.

Taxation had something to do with it, but not in the sense historians give to it. Let us analyze.

The same Tea Act that had **added** three pence per pound to tea shipped from England to America, had **subtracted** 12 pence per pound from tea shipped from India to England, thus rendering tea **cheaper** by 9 pence per pound.

Therefore it was not the "patriots" who stood to lose, but the smugglers. Who, not to fall under the long arm of the law, staged a masquerade: disguised as Red Indians, they rushed out of a Masonic Lodge in Boston Harbour, assaulted the ships, threw 342 cases of tea overboard, re-entered the lodge and vanished.

Complying historians do their duty by promoting smugglers to "patriots" and hiding the myrmidons of Mammon under a blanket of silence around the monetary issue.

Facts may be suppressed not only by hiding them, but also by distorting or misinterpreting key words. Let us see a case in point.

Embedded demographers point out that one of the reasons why a country like Kenya, East Africa, lags behind in development and therefore needs to control its population is that it has a shortage of arable land. They go on repeating that the country's arable land is only 17% of its total area.

The argument is interesting for hiding not just one, but **three** vital pieces of information.

The first equates **arable** land with land **under cultivation**. In actual surface area, 17% equals about 10 million hectares.

Of these hectares about half are under cultivation in all its forms, from small farms to ranching. But then, if all of this arable land was brought under cultivation, Kenya could support a population of 90 million, or twice its current 45.

The second is how the figure of 17% is arrived at. The 10 million hectares represented by that percentage consist of first and second class agricultural land, measured **exclusively** in terms of **rainfall**: in actual figures, 600-800mm (24-32 inches) per year.

Now 24 inches of rain/year can sustain a flourishing agriculture by irrigation, **if warranted by a high density of population**. The province of Granada, Spain, supports a flourishing agriculture on 15 inches of rain/year. Every drop gets collected and distributed by an ingenious irrigation system set up half a millennium ago under Muslim rule. If Kenya's all **truly arable** land was brought under cultivation, including the 44 million hectares of third class land that do not qualify in terms of rainfall alone, the country could easily support 360 million people.

The third and last missing piece of information is that the argument assumes **no improvement at the existing level of technology**. Were this level come even half way to the possibilities of modern technology, Kenya could support a population of **a billion or so**.

Is the distortion intentional? Again, we cannot say. The foregoing does not mean that it is desirable to have a population of one billion. It means that one should be wary of accepting an argument presented as "scientific" without questioning it based on easily available evidence.

Nothing but the Truth

Adding unnecessary or false details to something true is another way of confusing defenceless minds. Three examples of such technique follow.

You must have read, or heard, of an evil institution called the **Holy Inquisition**, with its Roman and Spanish branches. The following letter to the Editor portrays the common man's idea about it:

What about Christians persecuted under Papal inquisition? History records show that about 6 million Jews died under Nazi (atheist) persecutions and tens of millions under Papal inquisition.

Think of monks and priests in holy garments directing with heartless cruelty and inhuman brutality, the work of torturing and burning alive innocent men and women, labeled "heretic" because of their faith in Jesus Christ, by the direct order of the "Vicar of Christ."

The inquisition was instituted by Pope Innocent III in the year 1229 and became the most infamous and devilish thing in Human History. [7]

Ignoring the slip that in 1229 Innocent III had been dead 13 years, this was the first time I saw a figure in the **tens of millions** debited to the Inquisition. Soberer accounts have it that it imprisoned, tortured, burned at the stake or otherwise

---

7. Sunday Nation, Nairobi 7th December 1997. Punctuation and capitals in the original.

killed tens of thousands of people for the crime of religious dissension. In particular, it persecuted science in the person of Galileo Galilei, putting out his eyes before burning him at the stake. A milder account has it that he died in prison.

Reserving the understanding of the topic to Part Two of the book, here let us just separate the grain of truth from the chaff of added falsehood.

In truth such an institution existed, ran a prison system, and used torture to extract information. But it had no power to burn anyone at the stake. That power rested with the civil executive, not with monks and priests in holy garments. The figure of tens of thousands has one zero too many, that of tens of millions four zeros too many. It did not persecute people for religious dissent, but for religious **concealment**. The allegation that the victims were faithful Christians is too grotesque to go into. The Spanish Inquisition under the sovereigns Fernando and his wife Isabel, never molested Jews, Muslims or heretics who **openly professed** what they believed. If any of them, however, pretended to being a faithful Catholic while covertly practicing and proselytizing Judaism, Islam or heresy, the Inquisition, on behalf of the executive, swung into action, so as to ferret them out by interrogation (Latin *inquisitio*). These are the facts: any addition thereto is chaff.

The facts about Galileo are that he had a wrangle with the Inquisition, and that as an old man he became blind. The chaff is that it was the Inquisition that blinded, tortured and imprisoned him. He died in his bed, at the ripe old age of 78, and not in prison but under house arrest in his Arcetri villa in Tuscany.

Should you conclude from the foregoing that the Spanish Inquisition, or the Roman one, were not that bad because of the misconceptions about them, you are welcome to your own conclusion, but please do not debit it to me.

Another tale unduly embellished by true but impertinent material is the story of the American Civil War (1861-1865). Americans fought, as everyone knows, to rid their young nation of the evil practice of slavery.

Well, not quite. The facts of the case are that tension had been building in the first half of the 19th century between **three sets** of interests. Farmers west of the Mississippi wanted cheap land, railroads and loading bays along the great river. The northern financial-industrial complex was more than ready to satisfy them. But the Southern planters, **who also controlled the Federal Government**, lacked political will. They promised but did not deliver. In 1860 they lost the election to Lincoln, a man intent on developing the industrial basis of the Union. Having lost federal political control, the Southern States **seceded from the Union**.

For five months nothing happened, until the issue arose as to who should control a Federal fort in Charleston, deep in southern territory. The Confederates opened fire and war began.

After two years the outcome was still uncertain. To prevent the Confederation from getting international recognition, Lincoln passed the Emancipation Act of 1863, thus turning a political-economic conflict into an ideological one. Slavery had nothing to do either with the remote or with the proximate causes of the war. Some prints of the time portray Black volunteers fighting for the Southern army!

In time, ideology overshadowed all other issues, exclusively retaining truth status.

The last example of undue addition to truth is due to the complexities of war, art, journalism and ideology.

On show at the New York Metropolitan Museum of Modern Art, where it attracts thousands of visitors every year, is a famous Picasso painting called *Guernica*.[8]

The accepted tradition is that the painting expresses "horror of the bombing of this Basque town during the Spanish Civil War, horror of war in general, and compassion and hope for its victims."[9]

Now get a reproduction of Picasso's painting and **study it**. There is not one, but **two** paintings superimposed on one another. The original, still dominating the canvas, commemorates the 1920 death of Joselito, a famous Spanish bullfighter gored by a bull called Bailador (Sp. = dancer). The fatal fight had occurred **17 years before** the bombing raid on Guernica. *Bailador* appears at the top left of the scene, with the dead Joselito below, broken sword in hand. *Bailador* also

---

8. It is an enormous canvas 8 x 3.5 metres (24 x 11 feet).
9. Chamber Biographical Dictionary, voice PICASSO.

had apparently disembowelled one of the picador's horses (centre), an infrequent but well-known bullfighting hazard.

In 1937 the Spanish Republican Government asked Picasso to paint something for the Republican cause, and Picasso re-used the Joselito canvas by adding flames, explosions, horrified faces and assorted expressions of distress. The painting thus acquired an immense propaganda value, befuddling unsuspecting critics into interpreting the bull as a symbol of the Minotaur and of violence, and the horse's death throes as the agony of war victims and the like.

This is not to suggest that *Guernica* is not a work of art, or that it should be removed from the Museum where it is on show. The issue is that an undue superimposition has succeeded in distorting a piece of factual information. Whether or not the fraud was intentional, saying what actually happened would help people to judge for themselves.

You see how impossible it is to understand, and therefore to think straight, with flawed building stones, the pieces of factual knowledge. However much pleasure it causes to know the truth of things, it causes even more pleasure to put it together so as to acquire the awareness that only understanding gives. This will be the task of Part Two.

Characters of Chapter Two

CAESAR, Gaius Julius (100-44 BC). Roman statesman and army commander. Conquered and subdued Gaul and Britain for Rome. Was assassinated two years after being made life dictator. Few know that he was also a mathematician, philologist, jurist and architect. His reformed calendar is still in use.

ALEXANDER THE GREAT (356-323 BC). Aristotle was his master in all branches of learning. His ambition was to conquer the whole world not only militarily but also culturally. His disgruntled army forced him to return from India. He died in Babylon of progressive paralysis after a bout of drinking.

COLUMBUS, Christopher (1451-1506). Genoese sailor commissioned by the Spanish sovereigns to sail westwards to India. He landed in the Bahamas. On his third journey he actually landed on the South American mainland, but without realizing it. Died in poverty.

DRAKE, Sir Francis (1540-1596). Greatest of the Elizabethan seamen, he was the second to circumnavigate the globe in 1578-80, half a century after Elcano. Pirating on the high seas on behalf of the Queen of England, he died of dysentery in Porto Bello, Panama.

SOCRATES of Athens (469-399 BC). Teacher of Plato, friend of Xenophon and target of Aristophanes' witty remarks in one of his plays. He wrote nothing: his teachings are known through Plato's dialogues.

ERATOSTHENES of Alexandria (c. 276-194 BC). Mathematician, astronomer, geographer, historian and grammarian, was appointed librarian at Alexandria by King Ptolemy Euergetes. He enriched the library by confiscating all the manuscripts he could lay his hands on from ships calling at the port.

FIBONACCI Leonardo (c.1170-1240). Travelled widely to acquaint himself with Indian and Arabic numerology. He introduced the zero in arithmetic. The journal *Fibonacci Quarterly* and an asteroid are named after him.

MAGELLAN, Ferdinand (1480-1521). Organized the expedition that circumnavigated the globe in 1519-1522. After he was killed in a skirmish with Philipino natives, Elcano took command and completed the circumnavigation.

LUNN, Sir Arnold (1888-1974). Controversialist, journalist, writer, skier and mountain climber well into his 70s despite a crippling accident in his youth.

JOAD, Cyril Edwin Mitchinson (1891-1953). Journalist, controversialist, popularizer of philosophy and fashionable atheist until his recovery of belief the year before he died.

FERNANDO of Aragon (1452-1516) and ISABELLA of Castile (1451-1504). Founders and sovereigns of modern Spain. In the year 1492 they defeated the Muslims, expelled the Jews and commissioned Columbus' expedition.

LINCOLN, Abraham (1809-1865). Sixteenth President of the US.

PICASSO, Pablo (1881-1973). Talented painter who found there was more money in doodling than in serious work. To check, look at the frieze of the Barcelona Architectural School.

MINOTAUR, not a person but a mythological bull property of King Minos of Crete. It was slain by the mythological hero Theseus.

PART TWO

ASSEMBLING THE BUILDING BLOCKS: UNDERSTANDING

CHAPTER 3

FIRST LINKAGES

If you are interested in construction, you must have come across a structure called a **geodesic dome**. It is nothing more than a hemisphere built up of very light but immensely strong unit rods in a regular pattern. If your understanding is good, you should have already spotted where this chat is taking us. The title above, *First Linkages*, means that I intend to refer to something discussed in Part One, and the only thing discussed there that can be related to a geodesic dome is … have you guessed? The soccer ball. Next time you come across either one or the other, compare and contrast the two for a good lesson in understanding.

A cursory glance at a geodesic dome reveals a pattern of triangles. On carefully observing its design, however, you will pick out the familiar mix of pentagons and hexagons observed in the soccer ball. If the geodesic dome is a hemisphere, it must have the same 6 pentagons and 10 hexagons that you saw in the soccer ball held at arm's length: If it exceeds the hemisphere it will have more. Only a full sphere is covered by 12 pentagons and 20 hexagons.

The triangles make the difference. Why triangles? Unlike the soccer ball, inflated by air pressure, a geodesic dome must support itself. The **only** naturally rigid structure known to construction is the **triangle**. Each pentagon, therefore, is braced by five triangles, and each hexagon by six. 90 triangles go into a hemispherical geodesic dome, and a number between 90 and 180 into a dome exceeding the hemisphere.

There is more. The American architect who patented the design, Richard Buckminster Fuller died without knowing that Nature itself had designed the dome. In 1985 chemists were half-shocked and half pleasantly surprised on discovering a type of carbon molecule forming spheres modelled on the geodesic dome. In deference to the inventor of the artificial structure, they named the compound **buckminsterfullerene**. Eleven years later they were awarded the Nobel for the discovery. Do you see, then, how three **apparently unrelated** fields: soccer ball, architecture and chemistry, are linked by the **same** underlying idea?

Inquisitions and Their Methods

This second linkage regards the Inquisition, particularly its Spanish version. As you already know it **inquired**, for that was its appointed task, whether the people reported to it were single- or double-minded. The methods of inquiry, including forms of torture, were no better or worse than similar methods used in contemporary England or France, where no Inquisition had been set up. Whether we today have any right to judge the morality of such methods, now fully legal in the US and elsewhere, is a point outside the scope of this book.

The point here is to **understand the reasons** for its existence. In 15th century Spain it was State security. The State did not tolerate hidden dissent for the sake of political unity, and the State imposed death by burning on the impenitent false (because double) believers. Islam has no inquisition because it does not demand internal assent from converts to it. The reason why the State asked the Church to provide inquisitors was due to their experience (the Roman Inquisition had existed for three centuries) and competence: they were trained theologians able to judge the suspected behaviour of the accused.[10]

Why did the State need to do that? Insecurity. When the sovereigns Fernando and his wife Isabel asked the Pope to set up the tribunal of the Inquisition in Spain, not a quarter century had elapsed since their having cobbled together a medley of independent robber baronages into a modern State. The risk of religious disunity destroying the effort was very real.

So much for 15th century Spain. Back to our world, let us now ask about the origin of such an institution.

It was neither Rome nor Spain. The first inquisitor in history was none other than Moses, and the story of that inquiry is in the Bible for all to read. Numbers 25:9 reports the slaying

---

10. Let us add that the inquisitors Castelnau and Arbués, among others, died assassinated.

of 24 thousand followers of the idol Baal of Peor for religious dissent, a number far exceeding the victims of both Roman and Spanish inquisitions many centuries later.

It would be bad historical method if we tried to justify recent inquisitions in terms of the Mosaic one. But our effort at understanding the past can help us to understand the present. Let us ask whether, given present-day circumstances, forms of inquisition still exist.

It is of course no use looking for the term. You will not find that. But you will find institutions, on all levels and in all countries, ferreting out and severely punishing dissent. The secret police of the defunct Soviet Union, Third Reich, East Germany, as that of the not-so-defunct China and Cuba, as well as the intelligence "services" of "free" countries, are just that: inquisitions, alive and well into the not-so-young-any-more 21st century.

On top of that there is now the phenomenon of the **politically correct**. To express an opinion dissenting from the official line in matters of history, politics, etc., carries prison sentences in more than one country, prevents access to historical archives, forces authors to remove offending passages from their works, and otherwise to toe the line.

In North America you may find yourself sued by extremely powerful lobbies, each with its own inquisitorial department. Being condemned to death, executable anywhere in the world, is another fate that can befall anyone.

As this book is about thinking, however, I refrain from naming names, content with having brought into being some understanding that was not there before.

CHARACTERS OF CHAPTER THREE

BUCKMINSTER FULLER, Richard (1895-1983). Unconventional architect and uncompromising polymath, is one among many who became famous without a University degree.

CHAPTER 4

TYPES OF TRUTH

The purpose of thinking, i.e. putting together factual knowledge into understanding and ordering it by wisdom, is none other than attaining truth.

Avicenna, a Muslim philosopher and physician, taught us to define truth as the **agreement** between the mind and things. Truth so defined is also known as **correspondence**.

To accept such definition, however, is not an act of reason but of faith: in Avicenna that is. Followers of Descartes, like Bertrand Russell, do not agree with Avicenna and maintain that truth is **coherence**: a proposition is true if it does not contradict another. Followers of William James, like John Dewey, disagree with both Descartes and Avicenna, maintaining that truth is what works, an attitude known as **pragmatism**. It is important to grasp, therefore, that there is **one faith for each** of the three definitions of truth.

Why faith and not reason? Because the three positions do not contradict one another, so that accepting one of the three does not necessarily exclude the other two.

Correspondence, unlike coherence and praxis, is complete. Truth attained by correspondence is both coherent and practical, whereas neither coherence nor praxis guarantees the other two.

Mathematics, for instance, is the realm of coherence. No matter how difficult a numerical problem is, a solution may be difficult to find, but it exists. The problem is that the world of numbers and the world of things are not always the same world. When mathematicians fail to take that difference sufficiently into account, they may fall into the trap of believing that, given a mathematical model, there is a reality corresponding to it somewhere. And so they, and those who hang on their every word, come to accept such constructs as "space in eleven dimensions", "curved" space, "space-time continuum" and similar models as if they were "things" instead of the beings of reason that they are. They miss the ancient distinction between **numbered number**: the natural 1,2…n and **numbering number**: fractions, relative numbers, square roots, transcendental numbers and the rest of the fascinating array of beings of reason but unmatched by anything in the world of things.

It is the same with praxis. There is no denying that the principle of the fruitfulness of money, unnatural by definition, has been notably successful. But it has introduced the practice of usury in the economy, thus unjustly privileging minorities and impoverishing impotent majorities.

To sharpen your understanding further, think of a debate against an opponent. If the debate is conducted on the level of correspondence, both debaters are seeking a **common** truth. The proposer defends, and the opponent attacks, the **same thesis**. The opponent listens carefully to the initial piece of reasoning, shears off its rhetorical frills and reduces it to a syllogism. If unsatisfied, he rejects it: either because of a false proposition, or because the terms of the syllogism are strung in the wrong order or the conclusion does not follow from the premises.

The burden of proof is **on the proposer.** It is a sheer waste of time to try to prove negative propositions (such-and-such does not exist, so-and-so did not do that, etc.); this is a rule of thought, not one of debate: there is simply no method that allows such a feat. But if the proponent succeeds in defending his thesis, the opponent ceases to oppose and submits.

This, of course, is easier said than done. As Etienne Gilson remarked, it is not difficult to find the truth. What is difficult is not to run away from it once it has been found.

Be that as it may, the debating procedure just described guarantees truth, provided both debaters have chosen truth as **correspondence**.

If the two have chosen truth as **coherence**, they cannot but agree if the calculations are right, but if one of them adheres to truth as correspondence, the mathematical solution will not satisfy him. The mathematical agreement will not bring into existence space in more than three dimensions, which remains a **being of reason**.

The truth of a gang of criminals planning a robbery is the practical success of the operation; but that success disagrees with the virtue of justice, necessarily injured by their praxis.

In any case, if there is agreement on the nature of truth, there will be debate, if of sorts. If there is no agreement, debate becomes meaningless or downright impossible.

If two historians disagree on what trusted sources say, there is debate but no agreement. But if two scientists disagree because one bases his argument on proof and the other on testimony, there is neither argument nor, *a fortiori*, agreement.

In practically all of today's debates, in school or university, there is no real debate, and not because of disagreement on fundamentals or peripherals. There is no debate because neither side listens to the other, **by design**. Medieval logicians used to call this attitude *ignoratio elenchi*, a fallacy of what they termed "material" logic. Thinking of it, it is not a fallacy at all: it is a piece of strategy, for by not listening each side pursues its own argument, getting prizes on eloquence, delivery and support from "the floor". The truth or falsity of the argument is not even considered.

In the decades at the turn of the two millennia, the strategy has become increasingly obvious: the idea has been hammered ceaselessly that truth equals consensus. It is consensus that today determines political, economic and in general social decisions; and there is a sustained effort to make it work also in science.

But the laws of the universe are stubborn. Consensus on the "phlogiston" that accounted for the laws of combustion for 150 years was destroyed by the experiments of Lavoisier; consensus about the "caloric" fell through with the experiments of Rumford; and consensus about evolution, which has been hoodwinking the public for the past 150 years, is falling to pieces under the blows of chemical thermodynamics, micro- and nano-anatomy, and planetary catastrophism.

Obstacles Within

Ignorance and lack of love for truth are not the only obstacles in the way of attaining it. They are in good company with others no less formidable, all within ourselves, not without.

Consider **imagination**. It is an internal sense, confused with hinking by many out of sheer ignorance. To spot the difference, consider that whatever can be imagined (made an image of) can also be thought of, but not vice versa. Many ideas are thinkable but not imaginable.

For example, take the idea of **number**; whether numbered or numbering is irrelevant in this context. What can be imagined is not number as such, but a **number of things**: two trees, three houses, etc. We can also imagine the **symbols** for such numbers, but there is nothing sacrosanct about "2" being the symbol for "two", "3" for "three" etc. In the binary (base two) system, the symbol 2 does not exist. The symbol 10 (one-zero) stands for two and 11 (one-one) for three. Elsewhere the correspondence symbol - number varies according to the base.

Imagination exists to **help** thinking, not to replace it. With ideas abstracted from matter, the lowest level of being, imagination certainly helps thinking. The higher the level of being, the more of a hindrance imagination becomes to thinking; in the higher levels of spirit, with such concepts as will, mind, beauty, justice, grace, God, etc. imagination becomes not only useless but also an obstacle leading to error.

The mind abstracts from reality by making use, knowingly or not, of Aristotle's ten categories of entity. The "degrees" of abstraction are steps into, within, between and beyond the ten categories, the study of which belongs to metaphysics more than to logic.

Specialization is another subtle obstacle in the way of understanding. Pundits for State education have imposed on the school system what is in reality a characteristic of the world of insects. Without wanting to judge whether the move was in ignorance or deliberate, let us note that the specialist, who knows a lot about one thing, is prevented from understanding by definition: to practice understanding one must see the connection between at least **two** things.

The aircraft is an example from modern history. The Wright brothers were bicycle mechanics, but no bicycle specialists. They understood that the wind-tunnel data **calcu-**

lated by specialists were all wrong. So they built their own tunnel and calculated the data anew.

Prof. Simon Newcomb, an academic relying on the official wind tunnel data, "predicted" that a heavier-than-air craft would never fly. The Wrights, relying on their self-calculated data from their self-made tunnel, flew barely six months after the Professor's "prediction".

Bad will is perhaps the most formidable obstacle in the way of understanding. It is of course rash to ascribe bad will to anyone, but when a mistake is repeated umpteen times without the slightest attempt at rectifying, the suspicion of bad will is very strong.

The machine-gun was about ten years older than the young men who handled it on the battlefields of World War One. It did not take more than a couple of days of futile (and fatal) attacks against enemy trenches to realize how murderous its fire was. And yet, generals persisted in hurling their men against machine guns in their tens of thousands, to see them being mowed down like ripe wheat. **One million** young men lost their lives in an area no bigger than the London parks over a period of **three long years!**

Politicians were no better: they promoted and decorated the generals and **hid the news** of the slaughter from the public. It was only in 1916 that the British became aware of the need for a weapon against the machine-gun, and invented the tank.

When millions not of lives, but of livelihoods are at stake, bad will may perpetuate obvious mistakes for decades, as can be verified in 20th century economic history of Argentina.

Until 1935 Argentina enjoyed stability and sustained economic growth despite the Great Depression of the 1930s after the First World War.

That year the Central Bank was set up, allegedly "to stabilize the purchasing power of the currency and to avoid inflation", the eternal mantra that hoodwinks the public into believing exactly the opposite of what happens.

The results speak for themselves: the average inflation was 53% in 80 years, which caused a debauching of the currency from which it is yet to recover. The "investments" of speculators were given priority over the needs of the people.

Had this situation lasted four-five years before being rectified, the term "mistake" would be justified; but it has lasted 80 years, a very long lifetime. To add insult to injury, political instability went hand in hand with the economic one.

It would be as rash to dub Presidents, Ministers and Central Bank Governors dull and incompetent as to accuse them of wholesale bad will. But a good dose of the latter must have had a lot to do with the disorder. Showing it up is the task of this book; naming names is not.

A last but by no means least obstacle in the way of the truth is vice, particularly gluttony and lust. When the awesome power to procreate life is put at the service of its natural aim, the result is enhanced love, mutual support and self-sacrifice where and when needed; when it is given loose rein, its results are just as awesome; perhaps more so, but in the opposite direction. Darkening of the mind and weakening of the will are followed hot on the heels by others no less degrading but not worth spelling out in this book.

False Cause: Structural Thinking

For the better part of 200 years, clear thinking has been plagued by the revolutionary illusion: tear down the existing **structures**, replace them with faultless ones, and paradise on earth will be yours for the asking.

The first alarm that not all was well with the theory of structures was sounded at the Terror during the French Revolution, but *les philosophes* could not, or would not, see. The slaughter and mayhem has been a recurrent phenomenon: from the killing dungeons of the Soviet "Cheka" in the 1920s to the killing fields of Cambodia in the 1970s the inspiration has been the same: set up perfect structures, and people living with them cannot fail to become perfect themselves. The results have invariably, and perversely, been the opposite of those desired.

All of this is the result of refusing to see that problems arising out of flawed human nature cannot be solved by recourse to material means like money, law-and-order enforcement, "syllabi" of reformed educational systems, "deterrent" punishment and the like.

There is **no logical proof** that our nature has been deeply wounded by the **sin of Adam**, for it is not a truth of science but one of faith; the consistency of negative results from ignoring or belittling it has been so consistent, though, as to make its truth increasingly **obvious**, unfortunately for thinking people only. Unthinking ones are even planning to rehabilitate Pelagius, the 4th century heretic who denied this very truth.

An example of the futility of the "structural" approach is the drug war, inexorably escalating in terms of human and financial squandering of resources. If some thinking went hand in hand with the effort, it would not take long to realize that the most effective deterrent against the drug barons and their henchmen peddlers is not the forces of law-and-order but **lack of demand**.

Drugs of all types have been available for centuries, but as long as there was little or no demand there was little or no production and peddling.

Demand rose together with the loss of purpose, vision and therefore fortitude, of **people** intent on escaping from a purposeless life into a futile search for relief (of sorts) in drugs.

It stands to reason that demand for drugs would recede by strengthening the character **of people**, but current fashion wants the cake of a drug-free society with the eating of permissiveness. The blatant contradiction between the two is somewhat beyond the power of analysis of those who insist on fighting with the enemy's strategy and tactics.

Examples could be multiplied at will, but there remain a few more obstacles to analyze.

A widespread one is the argument *ad hominem*, directed at the person who argues instead of being directed at what is being said.

The lowest, and meanest, type of such an argument is the direct insult. Reviling an opponent and covering him up in abuse was common practice in pre-internet days; it is now attaining mammoth proportions in the so-called social (in reality grossly anti-social) media.

The most widespread of such fallacies is the phenomenon known as "certification". The surfeit of "pieces of paper" has turned such "certificates" into vague indications in the best and total illusions in the worst of cases. All they certify is that the holder, after attending a course taught by some "expert", has sat and passed an exam set by the same "expert" or by a "Board". Certificates do not guarantee ability to think, or improve knowledge required by the course, or talents in areas not covered by "the syllabus" and many other things that become increasingly obvious on their holders' doing real work. The only thing that the "piece of paper" guarantees is that the holder will entertain expectations beyond reason, and will be only too ready to hop from employer to employer solely in terms of better remunerations.

Increasingly, high qualifications are becoming the way not to higher salaries but to quick dismissal. Employers increasingly find by experience (after uselessly accepting certificates at their face value) that a less qualified person can do the job, at times even better, than the one with the prestigious piece of paper. The young graduate holder of the latter learns now how to think: Unlink yourself from the piece of paper and link to the work you actually do.

False Cause: After, therefore because of

There are people who deny that a cause must come before the effects it produces. I am not going to do that, but shall warn the reader that to come before a given effect is a necessary but not sufficient condition for having caused it. Perhaps, no one would deny that outright, but the temptation to link the unlinked remains strong. Consult any work of reference, including the Net, under the entry "Lusitania". It was an American luxury liner sunk off the southern coast of Ireland by a German submarine, and – we are told- the sinking forced the entry of the United States into World War One.

It makes sense until you look at the dates. The sinking took place on May 7th 1915; the US entered the war on April 17th 1917. As no war in history is known to have broken out **22 months after the *casus belli*,** there must have been reasons other than the sinking of the liner that prompted the United States to join the fighting. What such reasons were is beyond the scope of this book.

Peer Pressure

Let us close this section with one last (for this chapter: the list could be endless) obstacle to independent, clear thinking: **peer pressure**.

Consider first those at the **giving end** of such pressure. Insecurity can be easily spotted as the driving force behind their behaviour. Leaving aside the moral component, let us concentrate on the intellectual one. Such people know that they act unreasonably; they would lose that argument in debate.

Therefore they seek security **in numbers**. But the security of the herd comes at the heavy price of loss of personality and with it of freedom and responsibility. Therefore they put pressure on those who do not comply with that line of behaviour because such people are a reminder that there are alternatives, usually better, to theirs.

Those at the **receiving end** succumb to one single passion: **fear** of appearing different.

I am not referring to the kind of peer pressure you underwent at school; that is past now. It is the peer pressure you have already faced, or will face as a working adult, which sorts out the thinkers from the non-thinkers.

In this age when contraception is the politically correct behaviour, there are societies where it takes a brave woman to appear at the office obviously pregnant. She will be at the receiving end of ironic smiles, looks of pity, at times downright insults and undisguised hatred. Such pressure cannot be withstood simply by emotional counter tactics; it requires serious thinking, above all with oneself but also about oneself and one's family. [11]

---

11. Early in 2015 an Italian family caused a sensation at a TV show by appearing on stage with their 16 children (a national record). The obvious happiness on the faces of the 18 starkly contrasted with the looks of pique when not intense dislike of the interviewers.

In this age of perpetual and inextinguishable debt, it takes a brave and thinking head of a family to resist the pressure of not going into debt, living beyond the family's means for the sake of imitation of well-to-do neighbours.

Hasty Generalisations

It is always possible to fall into this trap. By simply omitting a qualifying clause or clauses a local, personal, or parochial case becomes a universal one.

In deductive, non-experimental sciences, it is legitimate to generalize even from one single instance. Pythagoras' theorem attains universal validity once any of its proofs is offered.

In the inductive, experimental sciences, even decades may pass before a "law" is proved not to be such, but to be an illegitimate generalization. From the development of taxonomy in the 1700s to 1970 it was asserted, with unfailing experimental pieces of evidence, that "all mammals have red cells in their blood."

That year, however, an entire family of Antarctic fish was discovered without red cells in their blood. That generalization ceased to be such, but has it disappeared from textbooks?

The worst type of generalizations consists of moral judgements of peoples, groups, or communities based on a number of unpleasant experiences with a limited number of them. Further experience may, or may not, confirm the previous one. The benefit of the doubt must be always accorded for the sake of truth (and justice that follows it).

CHARACTERS OF CHAPTER FOUR

AVICENNA (980-1037). Latinate form of Ibn Sina, Persian Muslim philosopher and physician of the Islamic Golden Age. He also wrote on astronomy, alchemy, geography, geology, psychology, Islamic theology, logic, mathematics, physics and poetry.

DESCARTES, René (1596-1650). Brilliant mathematician but defective philosopher. Bequeathed to the world the Cartesian coordinates and analytical geometry together with the idealistic (false) principle "I think, therefore I am".

RUSSELL, Bertrand (1872-1970). Mathematician, controversialist and self-styled champion of the logic of coherence over that of correspondence. Changed his support of social issues as fashion dictated.

JAMES, William (1842-1910). Psychologist and champion of pragmatism. "Beliefs do not work because they are true, but they are true because they work" is a recipe legitimizing anything up to and including mass murder.

DEWEY, John (1859-1952). Pragmatic progressive-liberal educationalist: "Democracy and the one, ultimate, ethical ideal of humanity are to my mind synonymous."

GILSON, Étienne (1884-1978). Thomist philosopher and historian endowed with immense knowledge and a high sense of humour. Any of his works is worth reading.

ARISTOTLE OF STAGIRA (384-322 BC). Most famous of Plato's pupils and tutor to Alexander the Great. Founder of the logic of correspondence. His metaphysics, logic and ethics are as relevant today as they ever were. His biology and physics contain much hearsay and unverified assumptions.

PELAGIUS (c.360-420). Hellenized form of the Celtic "Morgan". Monk who denied original sin.

THOMPSON, Benjamin Count Rumford (1753-1814). British scientist and technologist, who experimented with heat, showing that it was the result of motion and not of transfer of "caloric" as conventional wisdom would have it.

CHAPTER 5

UNDERSTANDING THE SELF

No formal classes ever taught you the supreme importance of the knowledge of self because it is not a "subject" that can be taught in a classroom.

"Knowing oneself", of course, is a way of speaking. What is really needed is not so much knowing as **understanding** oneself, so as to relate one's **being** to the rest of the universe.

As St Augustine remarks in his early work *De Ordine*, self-knowledge is another word for inner unity. He compares human nature to a circle. Unity means to see the circumference from the centre, equidistant from every point of it. The farther from the centre one wanders towards the circumference, the less united, and therefore the poorer, one becomes. For it is impossible to possess more of a circumference than the spot one occupies. Knowledge of self, as the following examples show, goes hand in hand with the mastery of self, starting with the capacity to concentrate on any endeavour undertaken.

Maturity

Self-knowledge plus self mastery can be spelled out in the single word **maturity**. Which is not, as many movies, games and other media would have it, getting money by any means except work, and ignoring the consequences of one's actions, i.e. behaving irresponsibly. The "rebel teenager" lionized in movies and shows can do what he does in a world where everybody else is **on duty**, in power stations, in transport depots and the rest.

Truly mature people not infrequently put their lives on the line. Dr Andrew Angel was the head chemist in a refinery of trinitrotoluene senselessly (i.e. without thinking) built in Silvertown, a populated zone of London. It was 6:00 p.m. of January 19th 1917, and he was about to go home when an employee came with the chilling news: "Sir, there's a fire in the basement." Angel called the fire brigade, giving them strict instructions not to let the flames cross the threshold of a store with 50 tons of TNT. He then asked the police to evacuate the zone as fast and as quietly as possible.

Then he could have gone home, but the **call of duty** kept him beside the firemen. At 6:52 p.m. an immense explosion shook the earth. All they found of Dr Angel was one of his hands. 93 people died, some vanishing altogether.

The Generation Gap

If parents and children think and act so differently as not to be able to understand each other, the reason cannot be other than that they live in different worlds. The parents' world is one of **work** to make a living. Uppermost in their minds are income, rent, taxes, school fees, etc. Children, on the other hand, live split between the world of school with its accompanying drudgery, homework, and that of endless (and mindless) **entertainment**, filled now to capacity by television, movies, computer games, sports, social networks, and the like. The brightest occasionally think, but excel at cramming textbooks solely in order to "pass exams".

Thinking is absent from both worlds. Rare are the families that buck the trend by fostering conversation, reading aloud, outings, developing manual skills such as repairs, building simple structures like dog kennels, etc.

Where children work for or with their parents, especially in rural areas, the generation gap hardly exists. There is continuity, for looking after cattle or sheep, wheeling construction materials or farming implements on barrows, gathering wild grasses etc. are purposeful activities that develop a strong **sense of duty**, i.e. responsibility. In such milieus teenagers would feel insulted were they told that they could act irresponsibly till age 19.

And here is another piece of observation: criminals are scarce among working people, but abundant among idle ones, regardless of the wealth they possess.

The only too real "white-collar" crime testifies not to the existence of criminals among working people, but to the largely non-work nature of what they do: paper-shuffling in public or private offices. This develops some virtues but produces no wealth. And more often than not they have nothing to do beyond drawing a salary at the end of the month.

That is where "white-collar criminals" come from. Giving a person false work, with concomitant security, is the surest way of perpetuating lack of self-knowledge. Without the challenges of life, and therefore without responsibility, there develops a paralyzing spirit of dependency instead of one of entrepreneurship and creativity.

The Overton Window

Today's world not only glorifies the generation gap, but also prevents it from being narrowed, let alone closed, by a technique known as the "Overton Window". Previously unthinkable, outlandish ideas are first re-baptized as "radical" and pulled into the window. After a while they are promoted to acceptable, then sensible, then popular, and finally to public policy.

The technique is independent of the quality of the ideas drawn into the window: true, false, beneficial, noxious, etc. The important thing for the window operators is the extent of public acceptance: superficial, half-way or deep.

The Christian faith took about 1000 years to be dragged into the Overton window. It has taken (and is still taking) time to be dragged out of it, at times successfully, at others not.

Some ideas, such as introducing justice in the economy by reforming the legislation on land and money, have never made it into the window, despite their desirability.

Ideas that have of late been dragged into the Overton window are abortion (de-penalized 1785 legalized 1973), animal rights (proposed 1894 being legalized 21st century), gender issues (1990 to date) etcetera.

From the foregoing it is clear that knowing and mastering the self are the only means to enter, or exit, the window about any issue in the exclusive pursuit of truth and goodness, without thoughtlessly being dragged in, or out of it, at the behest of forces not sufficiently resisted. They can be resisted, but the thinking, and the willingness, of those at the receiving end are generally too weak to oppose such forces successfully.

Semantics

The venerable Oxford Dictionary has an entry for "semantic" as an adjective: it is Greek for "meaningful". It lacks an entry for its noun equivalent "semantics". The recent Google dictionary defines semantics as "the branch of linguistics and logic concerned with meaning."

There is the rub. For logicians (of the correspondence school, hence with truth in mind) semantics is not a branch of logic. Shifting the meaning of words produces ambiguity and amphibology, gateways to falsehood and error. But 20th century linguists, intent on studying language for its own sake and not as a conveyor of ideas, have turned semantics into a branch of their "science", neglecting or downright ousting grammar from its lawful place.

In a little more than a century, semantics has acted as the most effective battering ram for breaking through one Overton window after another. It has created an asphyxiating atmosphere of "political correctness", now well into its being globally legislated (by thoughtless parliamentarians).

Semantics is, in politically incorrect terms, a trap. If you don't intend falling into it there is one, and only one thing that will empower you not to: **loyalty to words that convey truth, the whole truth and nothing but the truth**. A few examples will clear the air.

In natural law, for instance, rights and duties are indissolubly related. Man has an end transcending human nature; therefore there exist human rights, but only to the means to achieve that end. No right is absolute, but always related to a duty. Neglecting a duty entails the loss of the corresponding right.

Rights without corresponding duties are known as privileges. Privileges are not unjust per se: they used to be awarded to nobles (= renowned people) for shouldering **extra duties** (administration, defence, etc.). Privileges became unjust when the extra duties were ditched, again for whatever reason, but the privileges were maintained.

It follows that animals, without an end higher than their nature, have no rights. Thoughtless law-givers grant them privileges, necessarily imposing unnatural duties (and costs) on people.

The independent thinker will therefore wage a war without quarter against attempts at manipulating words, for giving in to such attempts leads sooner or later to fighting alongside enemy forces instead of against them.

A semantic counterculture has been laying traps of "politically correct" terms for people unable to stomach the plain truth. Semanticists deny that words have meanings, and that language exists to convey ideas. The overall strategy has been to convey the feeling of absolute liberty understood as independence from restrictions like rules, canons, etcetera. "Gender" has been uprooted from its grammatical soil to be pressed into service in the biological one. The blind have been renamed "visually challenged", as if the renaming could in any way enable them to see the horrors foisted on visually normal people by the enthusiasts of "contemporary figurative art".

But nature has a way of taking revenge. Even horrors need ground to stand on. Ugly buildings do not collapse; welded junk (dis)graces public spaces unchallenged; cacophony makes no impression on eardrums impaired by excess decibels. But not bridges. Have you noticed? There are no ugly bridges. The reason is not that bridge designers are particularly sensitive to beauty, but that they are **bound by the truth of things**. You cannot take liberties with a bridge. It must span a yawning gap and support moving loads across it. And what is true is inevitably beautiful, even without ornamentation. Antoni Gaudí's structures in Barcelona and elsewhere, in Spain, witness to the unity of truth and beauty in immortal architecture.

The politically correct trap has one advantage: specific targets of barbs throughout the ages can be re-directed to any group of people one fancies. Aesop the fabulist is supposed to have been a Phrygian slave. Some argue that he was Ethiopian: that's even better, for his fable about the… can be redirected by the reader to his/her own country/ethnic group/people/ etc. without offending anyone except him/herself, in impeccable political correctness. There it goes:

Long ago, Zeus entrusted Hermes with scattering assorted evils, lies, villainies and the rest equally among the nations of mankind. Hermes started travelling here and there, but when he reached the country of the… , his cart broke down. The…, thinking the cart to be full of untold wealth, attacked and plundered it, emptying it of all it contained. This is why the… are the greatest liars and evil doers on earth. The word "truth" is not even part of their language. I know this by experience [12]

For the past 200 years a basic, but crazy, idea has been stalking civilization: equality at all costs. Little by little differences have been reviled, belittled, scorned, and now downright denied. The modern State, in cahoots with the power of chrematistics, i.e. the idea that money equals wealth, has set up an educational "system" convincing its victims to be original

12. The quote is not a translation, but a rendering from memory. Those interested can find the people behind the… on the Net.

thinkers whereas their thinking is being increasingly unified by stealth. Woe to the one who dares to ask questions! He/she is marginalized without delay, which is the same as to say that thinking is penalized instead of being rewarded as it used to be.

In other words, we have a war in our hands. And wars are won or lost always according to the same principles: know the enemy, avoid his strength and hit him on his weaknesses. The text has provided, I think, enough of both.

Manual Abilities

The use of one's hands is a good test of self-knowledge. After hitting your thumb with a hammer more times than it takes to drive one nail into the wood, the probable indication is that you have no talent for woodwork. Fanning the air with a golf club more often than hitting the ball gives you a pretty good idea that golf is not your sport.

There are thousands of ways of using one's hands and feet, so that even a cursory list would not be useful. But it is important to understand that the learning of manual skills goes together with two other realities: **talent and apprenticeship**.

How do you spot talent? If you happen to have talent for some manual art or craft, the symptom is that you will **forever improve** at it. If you don't, you will reach a ceiling, a limit beyond which you will not go even after a hundred years of trying.

Apprenticeship has a tradition of centuries. Practical skills such as cooking, needlework, painting, operating machine-tools, etc. are learned best in a person-to-person, master-apprentice situation.

You may have experienced the frustration of being taught one such subject in a classroom, with a method that assumes everybody to be equally interested in and/or talented for whatever it was. The humanities: language, history, philosophy etc. lend themselves very well to classroom work. The sciences less so, and practical subjects not at all. Now you know why: the humanities, provided one has talent, engage exclusively the mind; the sciences require a mixture of mind and body skills, and the crafts a preponderant measure of body skills in which **no two people** are equal.

Imitation

Understanding oneself means also not to act for the wrong reason. A limited knowledge of self induces one to do (or omit) things for two wrong reasons: imitation and peer pressure.

Where young children live with working folk, they acquire a working lifestyle by imitation.

But when parents are absent from their children's life most of the time, which happens in urban contexts more often than not, the subjects claiming attention – and getting imitated – are television/movie stars, sports champions, flamboyant show talkers and the like.

This is not to say that such people are not worth imitating, but that you should not fall into the same trap as the *ad hominem* argument mentioned earlier.

What you should imitate are the **good things** they say and do, and not because of who does them, but because **what** they do is true and good, not false or evil.

The world of entertainment calls for further understanding. What is the relation between what the stars do on film and what they do in real life?

One hour is the average duration of a movie. In such a short time, and with many rehearsals, any actor/actress can afford to behave irresponsibly, stupidly, immorally, etc. as the script demands. There is no denying that some of these people have managed to draw the line between fiction and life, but many have not, usually with disastrous consequences for their own as for many other people's lives.

If you develop the habit of imitating the action, not the person, the action becomes yours; but if you imitate the person, he or she becomes your master/mistress.

Television

If you are not a TV addict, this paragraph does not apply to you. If you are, you had better begin to realize the enormous damage of TV watching on the powers of thinking, especially on self-knowledge. I am not talking about immoral shows, for which the remark goes without saying, but about serious shows, including so-called "educational" ones. Why do I say that?

Experience. The difference between reading and TV watching is both quantitative and qualitative. Reading supplies the written word **exclusively**. Meaning, scenery, sound, accepting or rejecting the thesis proposed in the book, everything else in fact, must be supplied by **thinking**.

Television, on the other hand, supplies **everything**, leaving the mind **idle**. Hence the overpowering sense of boredom after watching a TV program, **any** program. The worst thing you can do after such an experience is trying to relieve boredom by watching more TV, until addiction. It is the paralysis of thinking. This is not to say that television is intrinsically evil, but that its watching has to be done like drinking wine or spirits: sipped carefully rather than gulped down. Otherwise your dependency will prevent you from ever knowing yourself.

You need a good degree of self-mastery to do all this, but mastery comes **after** understanding, not before; if it is very difficult for you to keep away from the screen, you are addicted. But if you develop a reasonable portfolio of intellectual and manual abilities, you will give television its little corner in your life and never know what boredom is.

Play Stations

This kind of entertainment, non-existent at the first edition of this book (1998), has by now taken the world by storm, with hundreds of computer games that more than numbing minds poleaxe them every time some unfortunate youth engages in such form of non-thinking.

Let us see why. The difference between television and computer games is that the first furnishes everything, as remarked earlier. The second gives the illusion of thinking, by stimulating the user into responding to certain stimuli by appropriate clicks of whatever it is.

The result is an addiction far worse than the first. The illusion of being in charge, confused with thinking, makes the user seek relief from boredom by playing games often to physical exhaustion. The player fails to realize having been turned into a Pavlov's dog, salivating at the stimulus of a ringing bell when there is no food.

If this book succeeds in stopping the salivation of just one computer game addict, I will feel more than satisfied.

Marriage

Understanding the self becomes crucial when the time is ripe to take one of the most important decisions in life: marriage.

A whirlpool of opinions has been buffeting this most sensitive area with suggestions of all types, parading alternatives that appear attractive, but in reality destructive of the institution.

The basis of the argument of the enemies of marriage is that it takes away freedom by forcing an unnatural lifelong commitment on a man and a woman.

Arguments mistaking freedom for independence, which is what the detractors of marriage invariably do, are due to a serious lack of self knowledge. Freedom correctly understood is not lack of commitment but exactly the opposite. Committing oneself to a life of service, either in marriage or in celibacy, is the same as committing a locomotive to a pair of rails. Its freedom is the greater, the more securely it drags the train **onto and between** those rails. The only difference is that the locomotive has no will of its own; the spouses do. Living a commitment like marriage day in and day out increases self-knowledge all the time, for married life presents situations that are varied, tough and challenging. Tackling them with fortitude and solving them brings out the best in the spouses' personalities; living "partnerships" other than marriage fashions caricatures of men and women, tied to the chariot of their passions instead of driving it.

You will agree that the decision to commit oneself depends on understanding, before anything else, the true nature of marriage.

Matrimony according to natural law is not so much a contract between a man and a woman as a **covenant**. A contract exchanges goods and services; a covenant commits **persons** to one another who pledge their own selves for a purpose that transcends both.

The spouses confront Death, the Grim Reaper. Throwing the following gauntlet onto her (his? its?) face, they say: "You are going to take both of us, and we accept it. But we are going to defeat you, by leaving a larger and better offspring behind."

This talk can **exclusively be made** by a married couple, a man and a woman. It cannot be made by any LGBT, polygamists, polyandrous, "partners" or any of the neologisms pressed into service in the anti-marriage mode. Therefore the only cogent, effective retort to be made to anti-marriage people is "Very well then. Death is going to defeat you."

But the life of the offspring is **human** life, with an animal level supporting an intellectual and moral component. Whereas the first will develop anyhow, the second and third will not, unless protected and fostered in a **family strengthened by the bond of marriage**.

Two reasons can be offered for this viewpoint. The first is that the unity, stability and love needed for personal development exist only in such an environment.

The second reason is that the organization (division of labour, law and order, hierarchy etc.) needed to live in society, prepares the newborn to social life with a full array of family services to be seen later expanded to social services: first lodging, first school, first hospital, first government, first laws with reward and punishment etc. It is, in other words, a complete lesson in political science.

Its natural set up is monarchical. The father acts as head, the mother as counsel and moderator of political decisions, and the administration of justice flows downwards (distributively), upwards (legally), across (commutatively) and throughout (socially).

Entering the covenant of marriage with all of this in mind, therefore, entails setting priorities **inevitably at loggerheads** with individual whims and fancies.

Now it is time to think. As a married man or woman you are offered a golden opportunity (Ph.D. at a prestigious university, quadruple salary in an oil-rich country, promotion but in another town, setting up business in a very lucrative environment, etc.). Taking it would cut you off from your family for months or even years on end.

You would make more money no doubt. But it is a sobering thought that no one, least of all your children, will ever remember or praise you for that. If you want to know what they will remember you for, I have another real life story.

Years ago I attended a friend's funeral. Some of his children, who lived abroad, could not come.

His eldest daughter, however, wrote a letter, read before the congregation by his youngest. She gave an unforgettable description of the memories her father had left her. It was not his Ph.D. (he had one), his car, his house, his material possessions. It was the time he had spent **playing** with them, his children. He did not play children's games as a patronizing adult; he played to win, as one of them, at their own level. He lives on, as you see, in his children's memories. Despite his having gone, he was still imparting **unity** to the family, for unity is the unmistakable symptom of life, and disunity of death.

This is another reason why non-husband/non-wife unions don't work: there is no unity beyond the fleeting one of senses and passions, easily overtaken by more powerful passions as such arise.

CHARACTERS OF CHAPTER FIVE

AUGUSTINE of Hippo (354-430). Bishop, Father and Doctor of the Church. Converted after a stormy youth, he became one of the greatest philosophers who ever lived. Endowed with an exceptionally synthetic mind, he wrote 117 books most of which are still in print.

OVERTON, Joseph (1960-2003). American inventor of the deprecated window. Killed in an ultra-light aircraft crash three months into his marriage.

CHAPTER 6

LANGUAGE

If language is not correct, then what is said is not what is meant; if what is said is not meant, then what ought to be done remains undone; if this remains undone, morals and arts will deteriorate; if morals and arts deteriorate, justice will go astray; if justice goes astray, the people will stand about in helpless confusion. Hence there must be no arbitrariness in what is said. This matters above everything.
—CONFUCIUS

The above quote has lost not an iota of importance in 26 centuries. But what Confucius pleads is easier said than done. Consider the following questions: why is it relatively easy to learn a language as a child, but difficult as an adult? Why is it more difficult to write than to speak? Need grammar be drudgery? Are linguists pursuing will-o'-the-wisps in their analyses of language? Can there be a universal grammar/language?

I will not attempt answering these questions. It is my intention to give you a few tips that will improve your understanding of language, your love for it and consequently your care in saying and writing so as to be understood at once.

Words are clearly the keys of language. Words are related either to reality, or to thought, or to one another. There exist therefore three levels of language analysis: metaphysical, logical and syntactical.

Categories of Entity

The relation between words and reality is metaphysical. It has a most useful application in Aristotle's ten categories of being or entity, one of those pieces of real education that modern so-called "systems" unfortunately fail to teach.

The categories are **substance** and nine accidents: **quantity, quality, relation, habit, action, passion, time, place** and **situation**.

Aristotle defined substance as "what exists in itself and not in another". And he defined accident as "what exists in another and not in itself". Not that difficult.

Now note how the words you use every day fit within, between and across the categories, allowing you **to order** the ideas you express in their proper place.

Consider the word **market**: the first idea it conveys is that of a public square (**place**) where buyers and sellers exchange (**relation**) goods for money (**action/passion**). Therefore **market** is a term abstracting from four categories: **place, relation, action, passion**, with priority on **place**. If instead of **market** we say **the market**, as economists do, the category **place** becomes redundant, the other three remain and priority goes to **relation**.

But if we use the same term in the expression **to market** merchandise, the term performs the function of a verb in the category **action**. Etcetera.

Word Functions

You see then that the same word **market** can have three different functions in its relations with reality. Examples are virtually infinite, so you realize how important such mental gymnastics are. Chances are, however, that school (primary, secondary of university) has paid no attention to it, thus crippling many in their use of language.

There is more. In the foregoing examples I have used the word **market** twice as a noun and once as a verb. But if I say **market forces**, the same word works now as an adjective, and if I say that a price of a certain commodity has been **market adjusted**, that same word **market** functions now as an adverb.

Nouns, adjectives, verbs and adverbs, prepositions, conjunctions, interjections and articles are what grammarians call **parts of speech**. In Latin the parts of speech are easy to identify by their form. In English they are not. That parts of speech should appear in some languages and not in others has led some linguists to **doubt** the very **existence of the parts of speech**.

You need not doubt. Not to fall into the same trap, look not for forms but for **functions**, and you will identify them in any language under one disguise or another.

Whereas the relation of words with reality is **metaphysical**, that with the parts of speech is **logical**, and that of words with one another, **syntactical**. In speaking a foreign language one tends to use the syntax of one's native tongue, not infrequently making a fool of oneself. But never mind; let us go on improving our understanding of language.

Etymology

Words enjoy multiple relations with history, geography, other languages and cultures. This multiplicity accounts not only for their spelling, but also for their forceful use and for avoiding ballast, i.e. redundancy, repetition and meaninglessness words. It is a fascinating subject, neglected however by modern schooling masquerading as education.

The knowledge of the ancestry of words is known as **etymology**. You don't need specialized books to enjoy choosing, using and correctly spelling the right word to communicate ideas. All you need is a dictionary that carries such information, and looking for it. Let us take some random examples.

In English, the words Arctic, Antarctic, carry an extra "c" absent from Romance languages like Spanish and Italian. To understand, look at the etymology. Both words originate from the Greek *arktos*, bear. The meaning now becomes clear. The Arctic is the Pole oriented towards the constellation of the Great Bear (*Ursa Maior*) and the Antarctic away from (Gk *anti*) it. The example says that, after all, English is more faithful to the original meaning (and therefore spelling) of the word.

As a second example take *cursor*, which you, computer literate as you are, effortlessly identify with a little dash or rectangle **running** all over your computer screen.

Well, *cursor* is pure Latin for **runner**, indifferently applied to a racer, to the bearer of a message, or to the slave running ahead of his master's carriage (L. *currus*) to warn the crowds to move out of the way. There exists a huge contingent of words originating from it, its primary form being the verb *currere* in the category **action**. The words car, course, cursory, chariot, current, curriculum, currency, career, carriage, and others that you will bump into sooner or later, belong to the etymological cluster around that single Latin word.

Eponymous Words

Let us pay attention now to a group of entertaining as well as educating words called **eponyms**. They are words originating from the names of real people, with claims to fame ranging from meritorious to criminal.

Diesel fuel, for instance, is named after Rudolf Diesel (1858-1913), the German engineer inventor of the homonymous engine. The cardigan you may be wearing at this very moment owes its name to the 7th Earl of Cardigan (1797-1868); hooligans that disturb the peace somewhere are the worthy successors of the Houlihan family, members of which used to rough up the South East of London in the second half of the 19th century; the sandwich you may enjoy eating every now and then is named after the 4th Earl of Sandwich (1718-1792). The list is endless: eponymous words are found aplenty in all reliable dictionaries.

Had you learned the language in these terms you would perhaps still enjoy looking into its nooks and crannies for tidbits of understanding like the ones just seen. But such information is not "examinable matter". And false education has shortchanged you once again.

The Classical Languages

The neglect of the classical languages, Latin and Greek, is perhaps what has most negatively affected your understanding of English, and with it the joy of learning it.

You may have been fraudulently told that to learn dead languages is a waste of time. It may, or may not be true; but the point is that neither of the classical language is dead. Should one ask: "Who speaks Latin and Greek today?", the answer is not "nobody", but "everybody". Every English speaker utters hundreds of Latin and Greek words daily, but without being aware of it because of that canard.

You are computer literate no doubt. Has anyone ever told you that the very word **computer** is Latin? And not only that; words that I can read right now on the toolbar: **File, Edit, Insert, Format, Table** just to stop at these few, are all Latin. Now take **technology, cybernetics, graphics, macros, style**, and many others. Did you know that they are all Greek?

It does not take much to realize that the knowledge of these languages has the primary effect of making one master English. Should you one day tackle Spanish, French, Italian or any Romance language, you would find them much easier to learn with a previous working knowledge of Latin and Greek.

As you may doubt my assertion that mastery of English depends on a working knowledge of the classical languages, the burden of proof is on me to show that it is indeed so.

The main difference between English and classical Latin and Greek (but also Sanskrit, granddaddy of them all), is that they are heavily **inflected**, whereas English is not.

In Latin, "I speak English" reads *anglice loquor*; "the English live in Great Britain" *Angli in Britannia maiori vivunt*; "the English language is widely spoken" *sermo anglicus amplissime utitur*; "to english[13] a sentence" *sententiam anglifieri*. The word "English" functions as an adverb, noun, adjective and verb respectively. The form of the word remains "English" throughout. The inflection reveals the function even without knowing the meaning.

It follows that the classical language are a **great tool to order the grammatical categories in one's mind**, and that is why it is so difficult to speak or write grammatically without a classical background.

I finish this topic with an amusing instance of a misspelling entirely due to ignorance of Latin. The word, as appeared

---

13. Archaic usage, only for the sake of example.

in a newspaper, was **concerntration**. It should have been **concentration**, but either the author, or the proof-reader, or the composer, or perhaps all three, were unaware that it originated from the Latin words *cum* and *centrum* (together and centre). The meaning is then clear: to **concentrate** means to direct all of one's faculties to a single point of attention. But they confused it with getting concerned (worried, preoccupied), which is not quite the same, thus turning the end –**tration** into a meaningless suffix.

By now you should realize that this topic could carry on forever, but all I wanted to do is to stimulate your thinking in a direction that one day may prove fruitful. Unexpected, surprising relations between words and many aspects of life are endless. Expect more ahead.

CHARACTER OF CHAPTER SIX

CONFUCIUS (551-479 BC). Latinized form of K'ung Fu-tze. One of the great minds of antiquity, especially in the understanding and teaching of ethical principle.

CHAPTER 7

THE POWER OF PROOF

Paper Sizes

Despite the modern emphasis on science and related knowledge, little of it spills over into everyday life. Disregarding reasons and possible blame, let us recover time lost by connecting some of the wonders of science to what actually happens daily.

Look at the following equation:

$$1/\sqrt{2} = \sqrt{2}/2 = 0.707$$

You may, or may not have seen it in your mathematics course, but you would probably be surprised to know that this equation affects your everyday use of paper sizes.

The A and B paper sizes respond to practical needs by adopting the ratio of the equation above. Why **that** ratio and not another? It is the **only ratio** to stay constant every time you fold a sheet of paper into two. You can prove that experimentally, by physically folding the paper, or mathematically, by dividing the length of the short by that of the long side: it equals 0.707 in both the A and the B paper sizes.

The next thing to ask is what the numbers A0, A1 up to A6 stand for. They express the measurement of the sheet of paper in square metres. A0 means $1/2^0$ m^2, one square metre. A4, the most popular size, means $\frac{1}{2}^4$ m^2, one sixteenth of a square metre. Prove it by multiplying the lengths of the A4 sides by each other and by 16. 210 x 297 x 16 = 997 920 mm^2, as close as can be to the one million square millimeters that measure exactly one square metre.

The B series responds to the same ratio, but B0 = $\sqrt{2}$ m^2, so that the sheets are bigger.

The Burning Candle

How much paper sizes affect you and to what extent is as trivial as it is costless. Next I propose to you an understanding of science the lack of which bites, if only a little, into your pocket. You will be amazed at how much physics and chemistry there is in a **burning candle**.

All candles produce only heat and light; badly made ones produce smoke, melt wax without burning it, etc., causing you to waste money.

To understand why, look at the wick: is it straight, long and within the flame, or is it arching gracefully out of it, its tip glowing at the edge of the flame? If the latter, the candle is well-made, for you are observing a double **equilibrium**: the first between wax melting and wax burning, and the second between wax melting and wick volume. Both are constant, for the glowing tip consumes the wick at the same rate as the wax that burns, whereas the intact part within the flame carries as much wax by capillary action as melted by the flame.

Now disturb the equilibrium: break the wick, or expose the candle to a gentle breeze.

In the first case, the amount of wax that melts will be the same as before. Can you guess why? The flame is **above** the wax, which is now heated **by radiation**. Radiation depends not on the volume of the flame but on the area of its base, which is what it was before. On breaking the equilibrium by removing half the wick, this is too short for the whole of the molten wax to be carried up it by capillary action; the excess wax spills over the candle instead of burning.

Exposing the candle to a gentle breeze (a violent one would blow it out) has the same effect. The flame, bending out of the vertical, radiates **more heat** downwards, melting extra wax and spilling it.

The equilibrium may also be disturbed by bad manufacturing, for instance by not centering the wick in the body of the candle but placing it close to the edge.

Now look at the flame itself. The chemical reaction between wax and the oxygen of the air produces, like all such reactions, carbon dioxide and water. But if the wick fails to curl out of the flame the reaction is not complete and soot, in the form of black smoke, will tell you that you are throwing money away (not much, true) much as an internal combustion engine does when belching unburned hydrocarbons.

Notice its colours: blue at the bottom, faintly covering up the whole flame with a thin layer. This is the hottest part, reaching 1400°C. Next there is a dark orange layer, the coldest part. Above is the yellow cone, increasingly hot towards the tip. The flame is hot outside because the reaction between the molten wax and the oxygen takes place there.

An experiment proving the low temperature of the inside of the candle flame can be carried out but with a Bunsen burner, not with a candle. Place a small amount of gunpowder at the insulated centre of a wire gauze; open the burner below the gauze and light the gas above it. The powder will not ignite despite being inside the flame; lower the flame until its outside touches the powder and only then will it ignite.

Now blow the candle out and notice a whitish smoke wafting out of the wick for a few seconds. If you apply a naked flame to the **smoke**, it will ignite the wick by jumping to it across a few centimeters of space. If left to itself, the smoke will not last long, for wax is a heavy chemical with little volatility.

In 1860 Michael Faraday (1791-1867) gave a series of lectures on the very topic of burning candles. They are a classic, which can be downloaded from the Net.

Chimneys

I assume you know how to light a wood fire. Were you to light such a fire in a chimney, do you understand what the chimney is for?

To light a fire in a room you don't need a chimney. You could light it in a basin or suchlike contraption, but then you would be smoked out of the room. So it is clear that the chimney's main purpose is to send the smoke out into the open.

What about the heat? That is where understanding comes. If you pile the chimney deep into the flue (its hollow conduit) with firewood, you send the smoke out into the open, but together with the heat. I doubt this is what you want. What you want is to send the **heat into** and the **smoke out** of the room.

And that is what the chimney is for. For every chimney there is a critical distance from the flue at which the separation between heat and smoke is almost complete. Anywhere closer to the flue, and you will heat the sky. Anywhere nearer the room and you will smoke yourself out of it, an equally pointless exercise but in the opposite direction.

Energy and Economics

There is a small economic jump between saving money by lighting candles and by lighting chimney fires, but there is a quantum leap in understanding how to save money in the use of energy in its various forms.

You may have been told at school that energy is a physical quantity measured in appropriate units: the joule, the kilowatt-hour, the horsepower hour, and others.

It would be desirable, wouldn't it, if energy was sold measured in its units, but in the real world the only people forced to sell energy in energy units are **the utility companies**. You pay them by the kilowatt-hour.

But if you buy coal or firewood you are charged **by weight**, and if you buy liquefied gas, or petrol, or diesel, you are charged **by volume**. But what matters is that energy in all its forms gets taxed, so whatever form of it you buy you subsidize someone's salary.

It is therefore hardly surprising to know that firewood is **the most efficient source** of energy available to anyone with even a modest amount of land on which to grow it **as a crop**. You don't buy it, and you don't walk long distances to fetch it. All you do is to cut it into pieces that fit in your stove. And if the stove is one built so as not to disperse heat, a small piece of firewood can easily last the whole day. A quarter of an acre, intelligently renewed, can supply the firewood needed by a family as long as the sun shines, even occasionally. Transforming it into charcoal makes it more convenient for transport, but you lose the heat from burning off the volatile compounds.

The only proviso is that in order to grow firewood you must use trees that **coppice**, i.e. re-grow from dormant buds near the base.

It is not possible to compare energy costs except over a reasonable time, say one year, but as a rule of thumb the energy content of liquid gases is about 14 kilowatt-hour per kg, that of charcoal 6.5 and of wood 4.4. But availability, transport, taxation and other factors distort the real cost in directions not always beneficial to the household. The thing to understand is that by owning land you can control two sources of energy: firewood and charcoal. Otherwise you are at the mercy of the purveyors of the other forms, plus those who take "cuts" for themselves and their cronies.

Energy, Speed and Crashes

Misunderstanding energy at the levels just discussed is a matter of pecuniary gain or loss; misunderstanding it behind the car steering, or the handlebars of a two-wheeled vehicle can easily be a matter of life and death. Far from me to suggest that you do this thinking while driving or riding; but I would urge you to do a lot of it well **before** that, so as to develop a clear understanding of the relation between motion in any of those forms and life and death.

Let us establish some hard data first. Contrary to a widespread publicity, **speed does not kill**. In fact, flying safely depends on it; it is lack of speed that causes an aircraft to stall and drop out of the sky.

What kills is **crashes**, the more surely the higher the speed at which they happen. But whereas many people have a reasonably good idea of the relation between speed and thrill, few if any have any idea of what links speed, energy and a crash.

What is a crash? Unscientifically (i.e. thoughtlessly) speaking, a crash is one of the three ways of stopping a moving vehicle other than coasting to a halt or breaking. But scientifically speaking, which requires some thinking, a crash is an exercise in **energy transformation**, differing only in degree, not in kind, from the other two.

Appearances seem to contradict this statement, for at the end of coasting or braking the vehicle is intact, but after a crash it is mangled from a few bent panels to unrecognition.[14]

The difference is one of **quality**. Quantitatively, the energy of the moving vehicle must be transformed 100% into some other kind of it, hence the importance of the relation between speed and energy.

If you are one of those who thinks that braking distance relates to speed, one day you will kill: either yourself, or others, or both.

Since braking transforms energy from kinetic motion to the heat produced by pads or disks, braking distance is related not to speed but to energy. And energy increases not linearly to speed, but to the square of its increase.

If your car coasts to a halt from 15 km/h in 10 metres, at 30 km/h it will not stop in 20 metres, but in 40; at 60 km/h, in 160; and at 150km/h it will take 1000 metres, a full kilometer, to coast to a halt.

Have you got the ratios right? The increase in speed is 1, 2, 4, 10; that of energy is their squares: 1, 4, 16, 100.

---

14. Not long ago a photo on the Net showed a car that had crashed after flying 300 metres off an Alpine road. The violence of the impact had caused the engine to shoot out of the wreck relatively unscathed. The rest was beyond recognition. There was no mention of the driver and his passenger.

Coasting and braking transform energy from mechanical motion to the heat developing between the moving parts of the engine, of the transmission, of the brake pads/shoes with the disks or drums, and between the tyres and the road. Braking shortens the coasting time, but the ratios as explained above remain the same.

And that is not all. "Braking distance" is measured from the moment the pads or shoes come into contact with the disks or drums. To this distance you have to add that lost by a) your personal reflexes, and b) that lost in the time taken to transfer the foot from the accelerator to the brake pedal.

Do not underestimate this time, especially when you begin to get on in years; a) varies from 0.1 to 0.5 seconds; b) is about 0.2 seconds. Let us see what it means in practice.

You are zipping along a highway at 90 km/h, covering 25 metres per second. If an obstacle induces you to brake, and your reflex is 0.1 seconds, your car will cover about 8 metres before the braking action begins to slow it down. If your reflex has gone down to half a second, your car will cover 20 metres still at 90 km/h.

Consequence: should a wild animal, or a darting child, or a drunk, appear suddenly within that critical distance, you will hit it **at full speed**, fully conscious of what you are doing but powerless to do anything about it. Extra load, on the other hand, increases the stopping distance in direct proportion to it.

After such sobering thoughts, let us consider the mechanics of a crash.

A crash reduces any speed instantly to zero. But a crash at 60 km/h is not twice as damaging as one at 30 km/h. By the same token as braking distance, it is four times as damaging. One at 150 km/h is twenty five times more damaging than one at 30 km/h, meaning a 99% chance of death.

A crash at speed kills because the energy of the moving car must be transformed into another type, but there is no time for heat production. The energy of the moving car is transformed into that of contorted panels, twisted body work and crushed human anatomy. Don't you think all this worth knowing, and above all worth **understanding**, especially if you are the driver of a public service vehicle?

It is possible now to draw some conclusions.

The first is that the safe driving speed is proportional to the maximum speed allowed by the car's engineering. If your car can do 120 km/h top speed, and you cruise along at 2/3 of it, say 80 km/h, in an emergency you have four alternatives: **slowing down** by braking, **accelerating** out of trouble with your 1/3 reserve power, **scraping through** if the obstacle is not too obtrusive, and **crashing** if it is.

But if you go flat out at 120 km/h, you lose the first two alternatives. The brakes will make no impression, and there is no reserve power left. Scraping through is not within your control, and neither is crashing. Your life is neither in your hands nor in your feet. Judging by the horrifying pictures one sees in the daily press, you are a goner.

Should you **have** to drive at night, the above argument becomes **largely irrelevant**. What determines a safe speed at night has to do less with the mechanics of the car than with its electrics. How far does the cone emitted by your lights allow you to see?

Whatever the answer, the safe speed is whatever allows you to brake **within that cone**. If you exceed it, anything invisible beyond the cone may appear suddenly without your being able to avoid hitting it.

All the above applies also to two-wheeled contraptions, with the proviso that on a bicycle, motorized or not, you crash without the protection of any body work except your anatomy.

Here the understanding is different, and it is that falling at 30 km/h and above, your head **will hit the ground hard**. There is nothing you can do about this. The head weighs some five kilogrammes, so that the muscles of the neck cannot stop its whiplash at that speed as they would at walking or running speed.

Continue the reasoning. At twice the speed, 60 km/h, you will hit your head **four times** as hard; at 90, **nine** times as hard; at 120, **sixteen** times; etc.

Hence never fail to wear a helmet. And if you are as keen a cyclist as I am, every now and then have a look at your brake pads. Their surface area is so small that their braking action is effective only up to 30 km/h or so. Should you go downhill at 40 km/h and beyond, you will not avoid an obstacle except by scraping through or around it. You are in the same dilemma as the driver at top speed. Repeat: **never fail to wear a helmet**. A helmet on the head of a cyclist, motorized or not, symbolizes not only precaution but also **hard thinking**.[15]

Now you begin to understand part of the reason for the terrible tribute to death paid every year by motorists around the world. How much of it is due to lack of understanding? I don't claim to know, but if this chat succeeds in avoiding even one single death or injury due to former misunderstanding, I will be more than satisfied.

Flash Floods

On April 23rd 2013, a group of students were walking along a narrow canyon known as Hell's Gate near Naivasha, Kenya, in the Rift Valley region.

They were having a good time, but the area had experienced three days of continuous rain, and hundreds of tons of water were silently making their way to the head of the canyon.

Their guide, an experienced local Maasai, heard the first rumblings of the rushing waters, and shouted for them to gain high ground at once. Most of them obeyed and scrambled to safety. Seven, overestimating their savvy and underestimat-

---

15. It goes without saying that any cyclist who gets hit with earphones on, gets what he deserves.

ing the power of running water, pooh-poohed the Maasai and went on walking.

Then the waters arrived. In seconds, a mighty torrent rose out of nowhere sweeping the seven to their deaths.

Such accidents are common in all the desert areas of the world, and all have the same common characteristics.

First: they are common, but not frequent. A given area may experience a flash flood at irregular intervals ranging from years to decades. Hence there is no preparedness when the flood arrives.

Second: a flash flood lasts an average of six hours.

Third: there are few or no witnesses.

Fourth: "education" generally fails to explain, and therefore alert people to, its dangers.

Some explanation is therefore in order, with the sole purpose of making readers think, reflect, and understand.

There are two main considerations about moving water:

a) its carrying power increases not with the square, but with the **cube** of its increase in speed. If you can wade across a knee-deep stream of gently flowing water, you will be in difficulty if the water doubles its speed. If the speed triples or quadruples, you will stand no chance.

b) Turbulent water provides no lift, anymore than turbulent air does. No matter how good a swimmer you are, diving into turbulent water is to sign your own death sentence.

The reason is that the ratio of speeds 1, 2, 3, 4, corresponds to carrying capacities of 1, 8, 27, 64 times. 60 cm of water rushing at that speed would lift a SUV vehicle and carry it as if it was an egg shell. Ponder the point and watch one or two videos of flash floods.

The Environment

This topic shot to the forefront of the mainstream media in the 1960s, to become one of the many "idols of the market place" where to distinguish truth from falsehood is a real enterprise. The idea is therefore not to develop a theory of the environment as much as to detect the sophistry of some of the arguments.

I will focus on two topics: zero emission cars and recycling.

Perhaps without realizing it (i.e. without thinking), extreme environmentalists seem not to take into account the unavoidable principle that energy is neither created nor destroyed. It follows that there is no such thing as a "zero" emission car. An electric car does not reduce the emission to zero. It **transfers** the emission from the exhaust of the car to the exhaust of the generating plant that must burn some fuel to produce the electrical energy used to recharge the batteries of the "zero emission" car. The desired reduction could take place in countries that generate power **exclusively** by clean sources like water or air. But extreme environmentalists are also dead against building dams to create water reservoirs. Wind and solar energy cannot generate the amount of power needed.

This process, necessarily entailing one extra step in the energy transfer chain, consumes more energy, not less. In logic this is known as a contradiction, and an argument tainted by **contradiction** is worthless.

Recycling in general, and recycling paper in particular, suffers from the same defect. Two steps from raw materials: processing-finished product, become three if the starting point is a finished product: processing to new raw materials-reprocessing-finished product.

There is virtue in recycling when the raw materials are located so far away that it is cheaper to recycle from local scrap. If not, the argument is as contradictory as the previous one.

When I say "cheaper" I mean not only financially, but also in terms of damage to the environment, which happens with recycled paper.

Paper, simply put, is a piece of tree taken apart and re-assembled in another form. Paper making, besides being complex and expensive, entails the use of some noxious chemicals. Recycling paper has to undo that process. But removing noxious paper cannot be done without using chemicals that are at least equally if not more noxious (to go into the chemistry would be beyond the scope of this work, not to say the ken of most readers). And since paper is "bio-degradable" i.e. water disintegrates it, the noxious chemicals leach into the soil and contaminate it. Hence the label "recycled paper" translates into "more energy consumption and more damage to the environment".

What about the "depletion of forests"? Satellite photos taken since the early 1960s show that the forested areas of Europe (of all places) had **increased** by 15%. The area of the Nile Valley has also increased, for population pressure has made it economical to extend irrigation further into the surrounding desert. Which brings us back to thinking: beware of false argument, as easy to pass as counterfeit currency. Knowing how to detect false argument should be easier than to detect false currency; but it isn't, owing to the defective logic.

CHAPTER 8

FOOD FOR THOUGHT
(AND VICE VERSA)

Enter most bookshops, and the cookery section stands out without fail. If you find the connection between food and thinking mysterious or worse, please ignore both cookery books and this chapter. But if you sense that there is a link between cooking and scientific knowledge, read on. Opening any cookery book at random, you find recipes upon recipes from all countries. In no time you realize that it is possible to cook a different recipe for every day of one's life without ever repeating oneself. So much for those who think that cooking is a chore! But that is not the point. The point is, as you may have recognized, that recipes constitute **factual knowledge**. They provide no understanding of the processes involved, and no hint of their purpose or relationship with seemingly unrelated physics and chemistry. Once purpose and relationship are discovered and appreciated, cooking becomes one of the joys of the world (as the pursuit of wisdom must be, Aquinas reminds us).

The End and the Means

Since ordering things according to purpose is what philosophy is all about, let us begin with the purpose of eating, which is none other than maintaining health by taking good care of **the first half** of the food canal. The second half takes care of itself whatever you do to the first, but not if you hinder its functions.

Food processing, or cooking, is the art (and science) of **maximizing the nutritional value of food**. The more assimilable the food, the less of it one requires; there results less tendency to overeat, thus lessening a main cause of ill health.[16]

Principles

In such a complex issue, three principles ought to be internalized before the interactions of sensible eating, health and well-cooked dishes begin to make sense. The first is physical, the second biochemical, and the third technological. Let us proceed in order.

Physics

The overall physical principle is the ratio between surface area and volume. Take a cube of side 1. As it has six faces, its surface area is 6, and the ratio area/volume is 6:1.

Now double the side to 2. Its surface area becomes 24, its volume 8. The ratio 24:8 = 3:1, **half** of what it was before.

---

16. I have discussed eating according to reason in my The Art of Total Living, so that I will not repeat it here.

Now go in the other direction, halving the side to 0.5. The volume becomes 0.125, its surface area 1.5. The ratio is 12:1, **double** what it was before.

This principle, so easy to understand yet so neglected in formal education, links a veritable host of phenomena way beyond food processing. Here I shall limit it to the latter.

Biochemistry

Don't be put off by the high-sounding title. Biochemistry here is strictly related to cooking, not to the biological sciences as a whole. It therefore means no more than how the two senses of taste and smell are affected by intelligent, dull or bad food treatment.

Taste is three things: the homonymous external sense; the subjective appreciation of food; and the objective qualities of food itself which make it attractive to the sense. Whereas the second is highly idiosyncratic, the first and third require understanding.

All that biology textbooks tell you is that taste can be split into four: sweet, sour, salty and bitter.

Which is perfectly true, but as I warned you at the beginning, many things are true but not **the whole truth**. And the whole truth is that these four basic tastes are enhanced by an **infinite** variety of **aromas**, which give each food its characteristic, objective taste. How important the sense of smell is can be gauged by its loss. People who lose it by a head injury or a sinusitis, find eating a dutiful chore bereft of pleasure.

Whereas cooking has virtually no influence on the four basic tastes, it has an all-pervading one on the aromas, to the extent that bad (i.e. thoughtless) cooking **destroys** them, leaving food as tasteless as experienced by someone with sinusitis.

If therefore your idea of cooking is dumping food into boiling water that turns it into an acceptable soggy mess, you have missed a large boat in your education.

Start with the basic four. They are not the whole truth, but neither are they unimportant. They are important, but not equally so. The most important is the taste imparted by salt.

School textbooks may have informed you that common salt is sodium chloride, formula NaCl; and it is true, but again not the whole truth.

Foods contain a large variety of chlorides, carbonates, iodides, etc., both organic and inorganic. But few edibles are salty enough to impart not just taste, but also savour, that appetizing tang given by salt **in the right quantity**. Therefore salt has to be **added**, as the recipe says, to **taste**, this time meaning the **subjective** taste of those who will consume it.

Industrially refined sodium chloride is not hygroscopic: it keeps dry. It has a long shelf life, but its taste is inferior to that of natural, richer, unrefined sea salt; or, if you live by the sea, to sea water diluted with fresh water again to **taste**.

Beware here of industrial substances like monosodium glutamate (and many other food additives), which lace many processed foods sold in supermarkets. It imparts a very attractive tang to food, but as it is not natural, the body refuses to process it, relegating it instead to what can be considered as an internal rubbish dump: the fatty tissues. That is why consumers of artificial flavourings and assorted additives put on excess weight despite fancy diets and exhausting, but useless (and expensive) gym exercises.

Whatever you do, remember that the wise use of salt makes all the difference between insipid and savoury bread, cakes, stews, salads and many etceteras. And **the earlier** you add it the better.

Both taste and smell help digestion; tasteless food hinders it. A watering mouth is a symptom that food is tasty, aroma-rich and that the organism is ready for digestion at the mouth stage, for which the Romans had the proverb *prima digestio fit in ore* (digestion starts in the mouth). Linking this information with the surface area/volume ratio discussed earlier, you know now why this is true: crushing any food to mash, reduces the time of dissolution in the mouth by increasing the surface area attacked by saliva and thereafter by gastric juices.[17]

Extra-corporeal Food Processing, or Cooking

Because of **simplicity**, intelligent cooking enhances taste, improves assimilation, cuts time spent in the kitchen, and saves **a lot** of money. Dull or indifferent cooking does

---

17. The ideal time lapse between ingestion and elimination of waste is about fourteen hours.

the opposite. Few things are more disappointing, not to say infuriating, than being served an attractive-looking dish which has obviously cost time and money, but where the ingredients all taste the same, and the nutritional value is gone.

Heat Treatment

The nature and uses of heat sorely need understanding. Heat energy is a form of random motion, applicable by contact, convection or radiation. Cooking makes use of all three, but the first thing to understand is that heat, however applied, is an agent of **destruction**.

The heat treatment of food is therefore an art, consisting in letting it destroy undesirable traits like the taste of raw potatoes, aubergines, etc., while touching as little as possible the desirable traits, chief of all the aromas. Roasting, boiling, grilling, frying, steaming with or without pressure are all forms of heat treatment. But heat is not essential to food preparation. If a foodstuff can be eaten raw, like carrots or cabbage, to submit such foods to excess heat is an exercise in futility.

Heatless treatment of food includes seasoning, pickling, marinating, fermenting, curing, candying and many others which human ingenuity has devised over the centuries. Let us therefore apply the foregoing principles to the understanding of specific foods.

Bread

If you have ever tasted genuine bread, you must have grown weary of the pap bought in supermarkets that usurps its name. What is the difference?

Both use water and salt, but commercial bakers use baking powder instead of yeast and refined flour instead of whole meal. The perpetrators of this bereavement of flour are not the bakers but the millers. They remove the germ and the bran from the wheat grain to sell them at premium prices to food manipulators who make breakfast cereals and like products.

Refined flour is pure starch, barely nutritious and utterly tasteless. Its advantage is a long shelf life, and it is immune from insect attack (that insects should find starch inedible speaks volumes about this evil practice). Hence bakers add chemicals to "improve" the taste and the appearance of the product, thereby pleasing the eye but adding no nutritional value. Commercial brown bread is often caramel-coloured white bread.

Genuine (unrefined) flour has a shelf life of three days, after which the oily fractions of the germ go rancid. That's why the millers of yesteryear milled daily the small quantities brought to them by the farmers, enough for their weekly baking of real bread, the taste of which is unforgettable to anyone who has ever eaten it.

If you feel adventurous, buy fresh wheat in bulk, grind it in a heavy-duty hand or electric grinder, make the dough and bake it (Internet will show you how to). Like the millers of old, bake enough for a week, since whole meal bread does not harden.

Is it possible to make bread from non-wheaten flour? Only wheat and rye can be turned directly into bread, for only these two cereals contain enough **binding proteins**. They act like glue, preventing the dough from disintegrating. To make bread with maize flour, blend it first with enough wheat flour to do the binding (Check on the Net for suggestions).

Coffee

The basic taste of coffee is a dreary kind of bitter, but its smell is glorious. That taste depends on how much of the volatile **aromas** are kept **within** it.

You understand, therefore, that some actions can turn coffee from a glorious to an indifferent or even to a hideous drink.

Coffee is obtained by roasting the beans (technically the cotyledons of the seed) and grinding them before brewing it. Over-roasting and over-grinding **drive off** the aroma, destroying the very quality of the subtle blend of taste and odours wanted.

Grinding therefore should be carried out **immediately before** brewing. As it increases the surface area/volume ratio so much, leaving ground coffee exposed to the air drives off the aroma as effectively as over-roasting.

Brewing extracts taste and aroma from the ground beans, transferring both to water. There are three ways of doing this:

scalding (not boiling) the coffee in water, percolating boiling hot water through it by gravity, or forcing steam under pressure through it, condensing it afterwards. Ingenious contraptions have been marketed of late that satisfy all tastes, all very efficiently keeping as much aroma in the water as feasible.

After coffee cools down, the best thing one can do is to drink it **ice cold**. Reheated coffee will never regain its former aromatic taste.

What about instant coffee? Well, focus on that word "instant". That is arrived at by spending on the coffee **beforehand** all the energy you would spend on it **now**. Most of the aroma is gone, and that is why it does not stand comparison with the freshly-roasted ground thing. What you **gain** in time you **lose** in taste.

Further to sharpen your understanding, let me tell you how a keen but thrifty housewife treated her guests to coffee.

Shortly before the end of the meal, she placed a couple of raw coffee beans on the hot plate of an electric stove. As she entertained the guests, the beans were charred to pure carbon as the entire content of their aroma wafted across the room. As the guests sniffed with anticipation of delight, she went to the kitchen and served instant coffee. They praised her to the sky, completely befuddled into thinking they had drunk the real thing.

Contrast the sharpness of her understanding with the dullness of her guests. They did not grasp that coffee in the air is no coffee in the drink. Those who do, immediately realize that if they smell coffee **before**, they will not do so **while** drinking it.

Spices

The foregoing applies also to spices. Overheating and over grinding drives off the aromas. Understanding the ratio surface area/volume, therefore, suggests the solution: **sprinkle** a modicum of spice on the hot food just before taking it off the fire. You will achieve better results with less cost.

Meat and Fish

The taste of these two foods resides chiefly in the salt-laden liquids they contain. Whereas marinating and curing require increasing the surface area to be treated, heat treating meat and fish requires the opposite. If you cut up your meat or fish **before** submitting it to heat in any of its forms, you have problems.

Take roasting. Charcoal burns at a temperature of about 1000°C. Laying small strips or cubes of meat or fish on charcoal fire will carbonize them in next to no time. But if you lay meat or fish in bulky pieces on a fire you had better know what you are doing. The searing heat will char the outside of meat quickly, but the inside will stay raw, for the insulating effect of the charred surface will prevent heat from entering. And if you lay a large fish on charcoal fire, you will see it disintegrate before your eyes, since its muscle tissue is not as firm as that of meat. How do you heat treat these foods correctly?

Take fish first. Some people like their fish raw, thinking that roasting is too violent a method to heat treat it. Grilling, which radiates heat **from above**, is a gentler method (many stoves have this facility).

As for meat, you want the inside cooked before the outside. A microwave oven will do the job, but beware: this contraption does not provide heat; it causes it to develop from inside whatever you put into it, in the process turning life-containing food into dead matter.[18]

A better option is to wrap fish or meat in aluminium foil before laying it on the fire. It will cook in its own juices without losing any. After cooking, remove the foil and lightly char the outside directly on the fire. The taste will say it all.

Consider now boiling. Water boils at 100°C (at sea level), one tenth the temperature of charcoal fire. But boiling water leaches out of meat and fish precisely the salts that impart them taste. Therefore **do not** cut meat or fish into small pieces **before** boiling. They resemble meat or fish but taste much like a shoe sole.

It is better to **simmer** the fillet whole, cutting before serving. The temperature of simmering water is identical to that of furiously –and uneconomically- boiling it.

Vegetables

From the viewpoint of physical principle there are two types of vegetable: leaf vegetables with high area-low volume and stem/root vegetables with low area – high volume. From

---

18. It would seem that microwave-treated water kills, instead of irrigating, potted plants.

the culinary point of view there are two more types: those that can be eaten raw and those that need heat-treatment. Therefore we get four categories.

One: leaf and root vegetables that can be eaten raw, such as lettuce, carrots, cabbage and other brassica, endive etc. Since, as already seen, heat invariably destroys, and heat costs money, boiling such vegetables makes sense only if you want to make soup with them, i.e. you want their taste primarily **in the water**. But if you want to eat them, the most counterproductive thing to do is to boil them in excess water. To spend time and money to produce a soggy, indifferent mess of unrecognizable formerly gloriously tasting leaves, is a practice on which I have already remarked. Vegetables that can be eaten raw are best prepared as salads, dressed in one of the infinite ways you can find on the Net.

Two: vegetables that cannot be eaten raw, such as string beans, kale, etc. Boiling them in excess water loses taste, money, health and time at one go. The nutritional value of vegetables resides primarily in vitamins and salts, and secondarily in roughage. Vitamins and salts are extremely soluble in water. Boiling leaches virtually all salts into the hot water. Dumping this water into the sink adds insult to injury. But they must be heat treated, otherwise they taste awful. We seem to be in a true dilemma: one option destroys taste, the other keeps them inedible. Can salts be kept inside while heat improves the taste?

They can, by **steaming** them at zero pressure while suspended **over** boiling water in a steaming cage: they get scalded but the taste stays. And steaming can be done in minutes.

Three: low surface-high volume vegetables that can be eaten raw include the stems of the brassicas: cabbage, cauliflower etc. Appropriate dressings can do wonders.

Four: a potato cannot be eaten raw. Heat treatment is in order. The potato is, botanically speaking, a **stem**. Arrayed on its surface, inconspicuous to the eyes of a superficial observer, are **buds**, which germinate into ordinary stems given the right conditions. What feeds the growing buds during germination is the starch and other nutrients stored in the tuber.

From the culinary point of view, the tastiest part of the potato is the 5-millimetre thick layer **next to the skin**, storing sugars, proteins, vitamins, etc.; the rest is tasteless starch.

The above remarks may seem pedestrian, but they make all the difference between cooking a potato and murdering it. Let us proceed in steps.

Given that the tuber must be heat treated, there are intelligent and stupid ways of doing so.

By far the worst thing you can do to a potato is to peel it. Just look at the results:

- It wastes enormous amounts of time;
- It consigns to the garbage bin precisely the most valuable nutrients just mentioned;
- It denudes the surface of the tuber, thus facilitating the leaching of salts, vitamins etc. into the water.

Boil or steam the potato with the jacket on. After cooling, the skin comes off by finger action alone, or becomes itself edible, leaving the taste **intact**. To remove the raw peel scrape it off with a hard plastic cleaning pad, but do not allow the knife to remove the layer below.

Seeds: Legumes and Cereals

The first thing heat destroys, and quickly, is **life**. The same intimate relationship between cooking, life and death holds both at the personal and at the food level.

Cereals are seeds meant to be ground into flours of different types. Therefore all cereals are seeds but not all seeds are cereals. In any case, all seeds are **alive**.

Life develops forces of its own when properly treated. By soaking seeds overnight before cooking, for instance, they are made to absorb water, swell and soften, considerably reducing cooking time. But plunging them in water when dry, water must now be forced into the seed by the sheer physical forces of heat and/or pressure. And heat and pressure cost money.

Stews

Dumping all the components of a stew into a pot to be heat treated is a common practice that turns what should be a crisp blend of vegetables, meat and potatoes into a mush of dead, unrecognizable bits and pieces of former plant and animal life. It is a practice that you, understanding now the relations between all these elements, will carefully avoid. As the optimum cooking time for each of these elements is obviously different, it does not require much to understand that those with the larger volume, like potatoes, should go in before those with a smaller volume, like French beans and the rest, and those with a larger surface area among the latter, the last. The aim is to have everything fresh and crisp in the end.

What about meat in the stew? Meat is mostly muscle tissue, which contracts by high heat even in death. It therefore becomes indigestible and tasteless. To bypass the problem, pressure-cook it before adding it to the stew, thus preserving the taste.

You have by now realized, I hope, how many aspects of everyday life are connected with one another. This chat on cooking could be endless, but there are limits even to the patience of the lovers of the culinary art, and this book is on thinking. But if I have stimulated interest in cooking as well as in thinking, I will not consider my effort wasted. It is time now to soar to the high spheres of the human intellect.

CHARACTERS OF CHAPTER EIGHT

AQUINAS, St Thomas (1225-1274). Theologian and philosopher. A great synthetic mind that said the last word on many philosophical issues. Incorporated the teachings of Aristotle into Western culture.

CHAPTER 9

UNITING FALSE DISJUNCTIVES

Human endeavours, barring acts of insanity, are due to reason; technological advance, whether of 200 or of 2000 years ago, is evidence of that. The typewriter, invented in 1843, begot[19] the word processor a century and a half later.

Material achievements, beginning in fits and starts, sooner or later **converge** into an almost perfect solution, marginally but not basically perfectible from then on.

For endeavours where the human spirit is paramount, on the other hand, things are not so simple. Inevitably situations arise where two apparently incompatible alternatives raise their ugly heads. Advanced thinking should bring harmony, but alas!, all one gets is tribulation.

Why should there exist such problems I do not know. But they do exist, and it is useless to have recourse to logic to solve them. Here is where creative thinking comes into its own in

19. The typewriter that "begets" the word processor is, of course, a figure of speech.

the form of experience, especially historical, and in the knack of identifying correct solutions.

This is not, as one would think, identifying the better of two alternatives; it is to adopt **both under a higher, transcending principle** able to force a lasting convergence on an apparent divergence.

Spontaneous v. Scientific Logic

Let us begin with thinking itself. This ability awakens, somewhat spontaneously, very early on, at times before the age of reason. A **three-year old** girl was heard asking her mother this most profound metaphysical question: "Mum, why are there things?", a question that the mother could have handled better. Unless obliterated by fraudulently so-called "education" the ability continues, equally spontaneously, throughout life. But the Greek philosopher Aristotle (384-322 BC) discovered and ordered the rules of thought into a set of books called *Organon*. For centuries it was used as a textbook of scientific logic, grounding pupils in its impressive array of rules, terms, propositions, the syllogism, etc. That book is still in print for anyone willing and able to master its contents.

Suppose now that you have access, understand and practice Aristotle's logic, and think of it as the instrument that allows you to soar above the masses. Contrariwise let us suppose that you are one of the masses, with no time for Aristotle and for his high-brow lucubrations.

Which is right? Siding with the scientific brand of logic, but neglecting its spontaneous aspect, you enter the world of jargon of pure philosophy, understood solely by the initiated. But thinking that spontaneous logic is all there is to thinking, you are likely to end up befuddled by subtle but fallacious reasoning, as many of the unwary find out to their chagrin.

Both positions are right. Spontaneous logic is a **foundation**, as solid as you wish but foundation nonetheless; scientific logic is the **building** standing on that foundation. Whereas semi-skilled workers can lay foundations, only master builders can finish the building.

The transcendent principle that accommodates both logics is **metaphysics**, the science of entity as such. The neglect of metaphysics has relegated logic to dust-gathering books in the shelves of venerable libraries, and the teaching of the most diverse subjects in the classrooms has transformed the university into a kind of glorified technical school bereft of unity.

Within philosophy itself there are many false disjunctives. Platonists and Aristotelians, for instance, have never agreed on whether intellectual progress is due to the systematic application of the rules of logic, as the latter maintain, or to creative leaps of the mind as the former insist to this day.

The history of education gives the answer. Human knowledge progresses **both** under Plato's and Aristotle's dispensations. Had it relied only on dry logic, discoveries and breakthroughs would have been few and far between; but if it had made exclusive use of Platonic high thought without the daily experience of systematic thinking, instead of discoveries and breakthroughs there would have been flights of fancy without substance.

Curiously, it was Aristotle himself who found the solution of the transcending principle, but in the *Ethics*, not in the *Organon*. It is precisely in ethics that a virtue shows up as the transcendent principle between two vices, one by excess and the other by defect.

In all cases the main drawback is that the solution reveals its full logicality only **after** identifying the transcending principle, **not before**. And one finds it not by cold logic, but by hot intuition, experience, the wisdom of the ages, and by reliving the creative leap.

The solution that transcends the false disjunctive has been termed *et-et* (and-and) solution by the Scholastics. The wrong choice of one of the two disjunctives is called *aut-aut* (either-or) solution.

Subsidiarity

A modern example of the et-et solution is the principle of **subsidiary action**, in short **subsidiarity**. Ever since the revolutionary events of 1789, Western society has swung wildly between extremes that brought no end of misery well beyond its confines. The disorder has almost exclusively been due to failing to find the principle transcending the false disjunctives of liberalism and socialism.

The first raised its ugly head from the deliberate destruction of the corporate State towards the end of the 18th century to the end of the 19th with the rising of the Trade Unions. As the word itself says, liberalism is exaspered freedom without solidarity.

Socialism, its disjunctive, is exaspered solidarity without freedom. From 1917 to 1989, socialism succeeded in numbing the intellectual and moral qualities of millions of people in the erstwhile communist world.

The solution, practically known in Christendom for centuries, but theoretically expounded by Pope Pius XI only in 1931, is subsidiarity, the principle stating that what the smaller social unit can do by itself should not be done by the greater.

That mental inertia is harder to overcome than its mechanical counterpart is proved by the fact that the very word "subsidiarity" took 60 years to make it into the English language. For as long as economists and politicians were at the giving end of their liberal or socialist cudgels, they took no notice of it. When they found themselves at the receiving end of the Brussels bureaucrats, they suddenly discovered subsidiarity. Better late than never.

Protectionism v. Free Trade

The debate raging between the supporters of the two practices is another example of a false disjunctive. The proof? Whenever one of the two is applied, someone suffers an injustice.

We observe daily that unbridled free trade hurts domestic industry, and with it employment. But we also observe that full protection is a licence for the domestic producer to foist inferior products on the consumer at inflated prices. How to solve the conundrum?

A proposed interesting *et-et* solution is **gradually diminishing subsidies**. An infant industry should not be protected, but subsidized, to enable it to charge prices competitive with those of foreign producers.

The subsidy, however, should **decrease gradually**, so as to bring the domestic product to the same level as that of the foreign one when the deadline strikes. If the domestic producer can do it, well and good; the country enjoys a new line of wealth production and the consumer has a choice. But if he cannot, it should get out of that particular line, not to force domestic consumers into subsidizing a parasite.

Quantitatively it is the same as to increase import duties gradually; qualitatively it is not, for the consumer is unduly penalized into paying higher prices whenever a domestic production line is set up.

The suggestion is theoretically interesting, but it has a drawback unnoticed by the proposer. Setting up a production line entails creating large numbers of vested interests, which once embedded in the matrix of the economy are unlikely to disappear when the target is attained. A full discussion of the issue would far exceed the scope of this work.

Faith v. Reason

Last in this chapter is the secular conflict between faith and reason. If you recall Part I of this book, faith is knowledge acquired by **testimony**, whereas reason acquires knowledge by **proof**. The important point is that truths acquired by faith in people are liable to proof in the long run, whereas truths revealed by God cannot be so proved.

The issue is a different one, namely that truths acquired by reason in science, philosophy, etc. may **contradict** the truths of revelation.

Here it becomes necessary to explain the difference between **contradictory** and **contrary** ideas. Two ideas are contradictory when the truth of one necessarily implies the falsehood of the other, and **vice versa**. The contradictory of "white" is not "black", but "non-white". "Black" is the contrary of "white": if black is true, white is false; but if black is false, the opposite need not be white; any other colour would do.

This difference is paramount in right thinking. Its neglect has brought a great deal of confusion at all levels.

It would be rash to accept a scientific statement as true without checking it, not so much against one of revelation as against one of another science.

When such conflict is raised, it generally boils down to creation v. evolution. But logically there is no conflict. Defining evolution, as Darwin did, as "descent with modification", its contradictory is "descent without modification", i.e. living things are today what they always have been. Creation remains outside the issue.

Defining creation, on the other hand, as "coming into existence from nothing", its contradictory is "coming into existence from existent matter" or that the world as we know it, including its living components, is eternal.

Hence sound reason combines the two positions into four statements as follows:

1. Creation followed by evolution;
2. Creation followed by fixity;
3. Eternity of matter and evolution;
4. Eternity of matter and fixity.

Creation and evolution, therefore, are compatible (subcontrary in logical jargon).

But, one may ask, is evolutionary theory compatible with the laws of physics and chemistry such as oxidation-reduction, mass action and the rest?

It may, or may not be. But this is not the place even to begin thrashing out the problem, with its many interesting ramifications. Having identified the level at which reasoning has to be carried out is enough.

CHARACTERS OF CHAPTER NINE

PLATO of Athens (427-347 BC). Real name Aristocles, nicknamed Plato on account of his broad shoulders. Pupil of Socrates and teacher of Aristotle. Did not write a systematic philosophical treatise, but a series of dialogues the chronology of which is still disputed. Founder of idealism, which gives priority to ideas over things.

PIUS XI, papal name of Achille Ratti (1857-1939). Librarian of both the Ambrosian and Vatican libraries, he was a keen rock climber in his youth. The Ratti-Grasselli route on Mt Rosa in the Alps is named after the two priests who made its first ascent.

CHAPTER 10

DEFINITIONS

There is more than meets the eye in defining terms. The reason is that whereas definitions are needed in logic, and the more precise the better, **arriving** at a definition is not a matter of logic but of an unfathomable mixture of intuition, understanding, experience and so on.

An added problem is that no matter how bad a definition is, it is never true or false. A definition is good, mediocre or bad, but continues to be a definition nevertheless.

Take the worst type of definition, the negative one. To define man as "not a horse" is true enough, but with such a definition one would not go far in the real world. A thing is what it is, but is not the rest of the universe; hence the uselessness of negative definitions.

For a definition to be valid there are rules to follow, but I will not bother you with them. It is enough to provide examples from real life to see how important definitions are and what to look for to craft one.

Let us take two definitions of the Equator, one from an ordinary dictionary and the other from a geographical dictionary. The first defines the Equator as

> Great circle of the earth equidistant from the poles.

To understand that definition we have to know first what a great circle is and then what a pole is. The same dictionary defines a Great Circle as

> Circle whose plane passes through the centre of the earth.

And it defines the poles as

> Extremities of the earth's axis of rotation.

The latter definition requires knowing what the axis of rotation is. The same source defines it as

> Imaginary line about which the earth rotates.

In order to understand the first definition, then, we must have recourse to three more, but that is not the only setback. A further question is, "Is the Equator, or for that matter any of the other Great Circles, truly a **circle**?

Navigating along it on a calm stretch of sea, it certainly approaches a circle. Walking along it on dry land, especially where it crosses mountains like Mt Kenya in Africa or Mt Cayambe in Ecuador, one would hesitate if not refuse outright to consider the Equator anywhere near a circle. A better definition would seem to be in order, but let us see first if a geographical dictionary improves on the previous definitions. It defines the Equator as

The imaginary circle, lying midway between the poles, formed at the surface of the earth by a plane drawn through the centre perpendicular to its *Axis*; as its centre is also the centre of the earth, it is also a *Great Circle*.

The italicized words refer the reader to "axis" and "great circle" as defined in the same dictionary, but as the point here is definitions and not geography, I will refrain from going any further. Let us attempt a better start, defining the Equator as

The intersection of the Earth's surface with a plane perpendicular to, and bisecting the earth's rotational axis.

This definition is slightly longer than the first, but a great deal shorter than the second one. It goes straight to the point, avoiding unnecessary references to anything imaginary, and acknowledges the jagged nature of the line. Further, it requires no previous knowledge beyond the axis, and includes all of the information contained in the other two. The intersection of the earth's surface with a plane passing through its centre **is** a Great Circle, and the perpendicularity of the plane to the axis guarantees its equidistance from the poles without having to say so. Eliminating one or another of the subordinate clauses, the same definition serves for any line of latitude, and avoids redundancy of words and information.

Geodesical definitions such as the above, even if not perfect, lead to some understanding. On defining features not just geodesical but meteorological, physical or chemical, a bad definition may impair understanding altogether.

This is the case of river deltas and estuaries. The ordinary dictionary defines a delta as

Triangular alluvial tract at mouth of river enclosed or traversed by its diverging branches,

and the estuary as

Tidal mouth of a large river.

Both are **descriptions** rather than definitions. The first is poor, in that it fails to include deltas like the Mississippi's, which are anything but triangular, and the second means nothing to anyone who has never experienced a tide. The geographical dictionary comes to a partial rescue with a **causal** definition of the delta:

Fan-shaped alluvial tract formed at the mouth of a river, when it **deposits more solid material there than can be removed by tidal or other currents** (emphasis added).

But it defines the estuary as

Mouth of a river where tidal effects are evident, and where fresh water and sea water mix.

The emphasized part of the first definition gives the clue to the real difference between the two types of mouth. A delta, whether triangular or not, is formed by the slow deposition of solid matter in suspension; an estuary forms because of the rapid removal of the same matter, whether by currents, tides, winds or whatever.

Now maps begin to speak. Rivers draining into the Mediterranean, from the mighty Nile to the modest Ebro, Rhône and Po, form deltas. Of course: there are no tides to begin with, and no currents to speak of. Wind action, however strong, is insufficient to remove the silt they carry into the sea.

But tides themselves do not form estuaries. The Mississippi, the Ganges and the Indus all form deltas despite draining into the open ocean. On the other hand, all British rivers form estuaries, the phenomenon being a good indication of the stormy seas around Great Britain.

The information contained in the second definition of an estuary, to the effect that freshwater and seawater mix, is poor, for a good definition should refrain from using redundant words. Good definitions help understanding, mediocre and bad ones impair it.

Ethnic Pride and Hidden Agendas

At times definitions have a hidden agenda, at others they emphasize part of the reality defined at the expense of other parts.

Take the definition of "highest mountain on earth." Everest qualifies provided that "high" = "above sea level", but this information gives no clue about the size of the mountain.

Everest is a rather modest 3,000 m high peak standing on a plateau 5,000 m high; summing up the two gives it pride of place among the mountains of the world. But if you are after size, even Kilimanjaro beats it, with its clear 4,500 metres jutting out of the East African plateau, itself 1,500m above sea level.

That is not all: for absolute height nothing beats Mauna Kea, in the Hawaii islands, rising 11,000m from the bottom of the ocean. And if we define "high" as "farthest from the Earth's centre", pride of place goes to Mt Chimborazo, Ecuador, standing on a little known but measurable bulge at the Equator in that part of the world.

The same thing happens with the length of a river. The Nile is the longest river in the world only if its source is that of the Kagera, a rivulet on the west side of Lake Victoria. But if you take its source to be Jinja on the Lake, you lop off 400km from its length.

Equally, both the Mississippi and the Amazon get demoted if the length of their farthest tributaries is removed. Then the mighty Yangtze, thundering down the Himalayas and crossing China to the Pacific, easily becomes the longest river in the world.

Unnecessary controversy and nationalistic animosity can also be avoided by defining terms accurately. One such term is "discovery". If "to discover" meant "to find", the revilers of Columbus and other "dead white males" of the feminist agenda would be right. Lots of people knew of the existence of those places before their alleged "discoverers" got there.

But originally "to discover" meant more than "to find". It meant "to make known to the world at large", and that explains a number of things.

To begin with, it explains the difference in mentality between the ancient and the modern world. From ancient times well into the 15th century, people of all cultures believed knowledge to be something sacred, never to be "discovered" except to initiates. This applied also to geographical findings: that is why Leif Ericcson and others, who found and exploited Vinland in North America long before Columbus, never "discovered" it in its etymological sense. It also explains why Columbus' name was not given to America: he was never aware that it was a new continent between Europe and Asia. Amerigo Vespucci got the credit, whether fraudulently we shall not bother to investigate.

The phenomenon also tells the difference between ancient and modern education. As Plutarch put it,

Young people are not containers to be filled, but torches to be lit.

Ancient teachers, accordingly, did not fill their charges' heads with facts as is done today; they threw hints and spoke in riddles, until the brightest among the pupils got the point.

Further instruction was from then on reserved to the brightest, lest valuable knowledge went to the wrong heads.

So much for "discovery". Let us move on.

Going Round

A famous controversy raged for months in the pages of *Scientific American* in mid-19th century, so furiously that the journal had to print a supplement to accommodate the bulky correspondence.

Stating the problem can be done any time. Take two identical coins (with milled edges for meshing). Rotate one against the other till returning to the initial position, then ask: "how many times has the rotating coin rotated?"

The readers split into two irreconcilable camps, one saying "once" and the other "twice". But they both missed the key element, the need to define the vantage point whence they observed the motion.

Without that definition the problem defies analysis, for the coin can be seen to rotate twice against the background of spectators, but only once against the edge of the other coin. Without understanding why, they were both right.

A similar problem can be set against a different background. If you go around a tree, on the opposite side of which there is a child hiding from your sight by keeping the tree always between you two, have you gone around the child?

There is no answer until the expression "going around" is **defined**. If it means "going north, east, south and west" of the child the answer is "yes"; but if it means facing the child's belly side followed by the left, back and right side, the answer is "no". The child has kept his belly facing the tree, hence also facing you.

All of which shows how important it is to sharpen one's mind before engaging in argument, however mild.

CHARACTERS OF CHAPTER TEN

PLUTARCH (46-120). Historian, philosopher and biographer extraordinaire, endowed with a truly encyclopaedic mind.

CHAPTER 11

DIVISION

The art of division is an exercise in wisdom, for it consists in placing the elements of a whole each in its appointed place. Whether you are a spontaneous logician or a guru of the *Organon*, you will not divide at random but will follow three common-sense rules:

- There must be one, and only one criterion (in formal logic **foundation**) for any given exercise in division;
- All the parts of the whole to be divided must be accounted for;
- There must be no overlapping of parts within the division.

A division will be the wiser, the closer its foundation is to the **purpose** for which the parts exist. The examples that follow will show what happens when the above rules are observed and when they are flouted.

Screws

You have an assortment of screws in a box and want to make sense of them for optimum use. How do you sort them out?

The alternatives are many: by length, by diameter, by the shape of the head, by the material they are made of, by the slot on the head, by pitch, by system and so on.

Any one of the criteria will do, but the wisest is by system, that is, by the combination diameter-pitch **specified by the manufacturer**.

The reason is that the manufacturer knows better than anyone the **purpose** for which he has made those screws. Each system, therefore, has a great deal of thought and experience behind it, and making use of other people's experience is far wiser than relying solely on one's own. And you will save much time, for within each system all the details are already in order. In the end you will know how to recognize the various systems: BA (British Association) M/M (metric) etc.

The only reason why I appear to be wasting time with a subject as uninspiring as machine screws is the following story, where wrong screws spelled death for many.

In 1966 a Viscount turboprop aircraft banked between Britain and Northern Ireland to effect a turn, but it stayed in a banking position without being able to straighten its flight path, and inevitably crashed killing everyone on board. On investigation it was found that one of the aircraft's PCUs (power control units) affecting the ailerons had been fitted with oversize screws, so that the commands responded in one direction but not in the other. Exercising wisdom is therefore important not only at the level of high flights of fancy but also at that of humble bits and pieces of metal.

Books

Dividing books in a library is generally done by author in the catalogue and by title on the shelves. But the library of Trinity College, Dublin, divides its books by **size**.

The foundation of that division is obviously **space**, optimizing which they consider a priority. But since the purpose of shelving books is not the same as reading them, there is a price to pay: only qualified personnel are allowed to handle books. You and I would do the same if we were to transport books in a container of any size.

Were **both** content and space adopted either for ordering books in a library or for shipping them in a box, the confusion would be indescribable and the waste of time enormous.

Nations, Countries and People

With books and screws the confusion would hurt no one except readers and users, at worst causing a limited disaster as happened to the ill-fated Viscount. Getting the wrong division in politics with terms like "nation," "tribe," "territory," "country," "people" etc. may cause rivers of blood to flow, as happened in former Yugoslavia in the early 1990s.

In such issues emotion usually clouds thinking. Clouding impairs defining, and wrong definitions end up in wrong divisions. Like time bombs, they explode at the appointed time.

The fuse that sets off the bomb is usually the term **nation**. This term, related to the Latin *nasci*, to be born, spawns also

native, innate, natural, and by derivation **national**, promptly exploited by political wisdomers calling State confiscation of private wealth **nationalization** in the name of, you guessed it, **nationalism**.

To place each reality where it belongs, we must first define this troublesome term.

A nation is a homogeneous group of people who think, act, speak and otherwise behave similarly. This was the original meaning of the word before its use came to be distorted in modern times to refer to political entities.

Let me point out that a tribe differs from a nation in degree but not in kind. Livy says that it was Servius Tullius sixth king of Rome to call tribes the fiscal (tributary) units of the city.

The Romans had even deified themselves as a nation, inventing a goddess and calling her *Natio*, so as to give a religious connotation to the affair. But since most people today receive no historical education worth speaking of, they are brainwashed into condemning tribes and tribalism as if they were evil.

Even a cursory look at reality should make such people think again. Why should the 20 million Igbo of Nigeria be called tribe and the 4.5 million of Norwegians **nation**?

The reason seems to be that the term **nation** strongly suggests **natural** unity. Therefore today's politicos, especially if in charge of medleys of peoples of the most diverse ethnic origin, love to use that term to connote the **country**, in the fond hope that by using the word the desired unity will take care of itself. That is why they are frightened to acknowledge the status of nation for any of the groups living within their borders, lest any such group get ideas of secession and independence.

Yugoslavia

What happened in erstwhile Yugoslavia is an example of the political consequences of faulty logical division. The Balkans (Turkish for "mountains") a mountain range in the homonymous peninsula in southern Europe, have been inhabited for centuries by people of the most different ethnic stock and religious background. Serbs, Montenegrins and Bulgarians are ethnically Slavs and religiously Orthodox Christians. Slovenians and Croats are also Slavs but Catholics. Albanians belong to their own ethnic stock but are religiously divided into Catholic, Orthodox and Muslims. There were also Italians, Romany (Gypsies), Turks, Greeks and others, each valley sheltering people of the same group sticking together as people usually do.

Until World War I, two empires ruled over this medley of people: Austria in the north and the Ottomans in the south. After the war, the victorious Entente consigned both empires to oblivion and invented Yugoslavia (= land of the southern Slavs), which they assigned to the Serbian dynasty Karageorgevich. The sovereign was a *de facto* emperor, but *de iure* he did not dare to call himself that.

The victors of World War II finished the job. They abolished the Yugoslav monarchy and assigned the country to a self-styled Tito, another *de facto* emperor who ruled over the same intractable medley of peoples with the stick of terror and the carrot of illogicality. The rules of division are meant to clarify not only thought, but also praxis. Tito flouted them all.

The first rule is that there must be a single foundation for the division. Up to 1971 Yugoslavia divided its people into a) Nations, b) Nationalities and c) Other Nationalities and Ethnic Groups. The division discriminated on the size of the various groups, but kept the single foundation of **ethnicity**.

In 1971 Tito granted the Muslims of Bosnia the status of Nation, thereby introducing **religion** as a **second foundation** for the division.

The unhappy territory had already been divided, once along linguistic and twice along religious lines. In the 4th century, Emperor Theodosius decreed that the dividing line between the Latin-speaking West and the Greek-speaking East should pass smack in the middle of it. In the 11th century the Serbs followed Constantinople into Orthodoxy after the Eastern Schism, while the Croats remained Catholic. In the 15th century the Ottomans converted a sizable portion of both Serbs and Croats to Islam.

As a result the same nation, speaking the same Serbo-Croat language, uses the Latin script west of the Theodosius line and the Cyrillic script east of it. It is overwhelmingly Catholic west and overwhelmingly Orthodox east of the line; on both sides of the line are the aforementioned Muslim Serbs and Croats whom Tito promoted to Nation in 1971.

Let us see now what Tito did with the second rule of division that all the parts of the whole must be accounted for. The Albanians, a real nation, were not granted that status; the Turks, overwhelmingly Muslim, were not included in the newly-created Muslim Nation. As a result he also broke the third rule, which forbids overlapping between any two parts of the whole.

It became increasingly difficult to pin down any given person to a given nationality or religion, for the possessor of any status was able to change it as the opportunity arose. The confusion could only get worse, and it did after Tito's death in 1980.

The fuse reached the detonator ten years later, when one nation after another claimed statehood and independence from what they regarded a foreign political domination. First went Slovenia, with no problems; then Croatia, who expelled the Serbs living within its territory; and finally Bosnia, with the horrors we all know.

Which goes to show that disorder in the mind begets disorder in the will; then the disorder spills over into society, and eventually explodes into armed conflict.

Clarifying the division also avoids loose talk such as:

- Talking of "nation building" without realizing it is an oxymoron or contradiction in terms. Nature builds nations, not politics; but throughout history empires have always tried to cobble together groups of nations into one country.

- Confusing nationality with citizenship. The second can be changed; the first cannot, anymore than the spots of a leopard can be washed off with detergent.

- Taking the United Nations seriously. Real nations, i.e. homogeneous ethnic units, are completely **unrepresented** in that organization. Governments are, some much more than others, which makes a mockery of the very democracy they peddle everywhere.

- Misreading maps as if each border enclosed a single nation. Erstwhile Czechoslovakia, for instance, was not made of non-existent Czechoslovakians, but of Czechs, Slovaks, Germans, Hungarians, Poles and Ruthenians. The United States respond to a different criterion: members of immigrant nations were uprooted from their ancestral lands, so that it was easier to instal them together in that immense territory.

- Insisting on the inevitability of the Nation-State. That a nation is a natural unit does not necessarily mean that it should aspire to statehood, governed by a central authority that wields power over all the groups making it up. The Somalis are a very good example. This nation is ancestrally divided into clans, all fiercely independent of one another and rejecting to be ruled as one political whole by any of them. Those who try to impose the Western idea of Nation-State on such people do so at their own peril, as the Italians learned during the colonial period and the Americans from 1993 to date.

I fully accept that the meaning of the word **nation** has changed in practice. I am only chatting on thinking, which entails exposing the consequences of giving words meanings that they were not intended to have.

The Living World

The time-honoured classification of living organisms into Phyla, Classes, Orders, Families, Genera and Species has suffered the same fate as ex-Yugoslavia.

Linnaeus introduced a binomial system of plant and animal nomenclature on a single foundation: form. But following transformist (evolutionary) theorizing by Darwin, Spencer and others, foundations other than form entered classification, bringing into existence thousands of groups by giving "evolutionary significance" to obscure anatomical, physiological, embryological or even ecological details.

As a result, groups have increased and multiplied beyond the grasp of specialists and non-specialists alike, with confusion, overlapping and duplication increasing by the day.

CHARACTERS OF CHAPTER ELEVEN

LIVY, properly Titus Livius (59 BC–17 AD). Author of a monumental History of Rome in 142 volumes, only 35 of which are extant. Worked for Emperor Augustus without ever consenting to flattery.

KARAGEORGEVICH. Serbian dynasty founded by "Black George" a Serb who sought independence from Ottoman rule. The original George is reputed to have killed 125 men by his own hand. The dynasty came to an end in 1945.

TITO, Josip Broz (1892-1980). According to one story, Tito was the *nom de guerre* of Josip Broz. According to another story his real name was Josip Walter Weiss. With his British-equipped army he massacred thousands of assorted Croats, Germans and Italians.

THEODOSIUS the Great (346-395). Roman emperor of the East during some of the stormiest times for the Empire.

LINNAEUS (1707-1778). Latinized name of Carl Linné, Swedish botanist who invented the binomial system of classification for living organisms.

DARWIN, Charles Robert (1809-1882). Inventor of natural selection by which he thought new species would originate. But species, stubbornly, reject change as much as chemical elements reject theirs.

SPENCER, Herbert (1820-1903). Railway engineer turned evolutionary philosopher and propagandist. Actual inventor of the term "evolution".

CHAPTER 12

THINKING TOOLS

Everyday language can play tricks on our thinking. The fact is that the human mind can produce ideas at a much greater rate than it produces matching words for each idea. A word may therefore convey more than one idea, or a given language may lack a word for a certain idea or one idea may be represented by more than one word etc.

All of this naturally begets confusion. Clear thinking requires that a given idea be conveyed by the same word throughout one's use of it, whether alone or in company. There are several thinking tools to achieve this one-to-one correspondence.

Distinction

To distinguish means to tell apart ideas falsely or wrongly kept together by defective language, by lazy thinking, or both.

A necessary distinction, in any society of any size, is that between an office and its holder. It is a constant of history that people in low as in high office are not exempt from personal defects; but it does not follow that an office should be blamed for that, much less done away with. To do so would be like advocating the disintegration of society, by abolishing all offices!

Another necessary distinction is between what is possible and what is desirable. Herodotus informs us that armies of women (the Amazons) are possible. But are they desirable?

George Bernard Shaw remarked:

> The exemption of women from military service is founded not in any natural inaptitude that men do not share, but on the fact that communities cannot reproduce themselves without plenty of women. Men are more largely dispensable, and are sacrificed accordingly.[20]

History bears this out. What won the Second Punic War for Rome were not its men but its women, despite their absence from the battlefield. Hannibal's army had invaded Italy 19 years earlier. He was therefore far away from Carthage and fresh supplies of young recruits. Rome lost all the engagements against the Carthaginians on Italian soil, but every fighting season young fresh troops went to thicken the ranks of the Roman army, until Scipio could bring war to Carthage's home ground, where he won a decisive battle at Zama in 202 BC.

But the lessons of history are lost on our contemporaries, who insist on having the cake of child bearing and nurtur-

---

20. *Saint Joan*, preface

ing mothers at home and eating that of fighting ones on the battlefield. There's very little one can do other than wishing them luck.

Analogy

Analogy consists in using ideas from one level of being to illustrate or clarify ideas from another level. It is a most useful tool, especially when the idea used is transferred from a more familiar to a less familiar realm. Badly used, though, it can become a bedeviling tool of confusion. The problem is that analogy **helps** to think clearly, but it **proves nothing**. A few examples will bring the point home.

In analogy of **reference**, an idea taken from a certain realm of reality is used for another. To say that a certain place has a "healthy" climate is, strictly speaking, meaningless: only living things are, or are not, healthy. But it helps to think that by living in such a climate one's health may benefit. But, to call trade competition "healthy" if you benefit from it, and "unhealthy" if someone else does, shows the shortcomings of this analogy of reference.

In analogy of **divergence** an idea from one realm of reality is used in **another**. The term **time**, for instance, can refer to present, past and future as much as to the movement of a clock. But the perception of present, past and future is psychological: the first is awareness, the second memory and the third imagination. None is a quantity, and therefore none is measurable. A clock is a measuring contraption, but not of time: it measures exactly its own motion, constructed as to coincide more or less accurately with the motions of the Earth.

Parables, allegories, metaphors and all types of **incomplete comparisons** are also analogies. I used a metaphor at the beginning of this book, when comparing factual knowledge, understanding and wisdom to the construction of a building. But thinking, of course, does not end as a building does. It is a means to achieve truth. Analogies enliven prose in speech and in dialogue, but in serious argument a bad analogy may justify anything.

Felix Dzerzhinsky, the head of the CHEKA, Lenin's secret police, used to argue that he was not shooting innocent people in his dungeons, but enemy soldiers fighting a war.

The analogy of war clearly went too far. In battle you do not distinguish between enemy soldiers, because you cannot. In a prison you can, and it is your duty to arraign them before courts of law to determine guilt if any.

Birth-control advocates ("family planning experts" in today's politically correct term), from contraceptive peddlers to AIDS campaigners, are fond of metaphors like

> If it right for a man to use an umbrella to protect himself from rain, why should it not be right to use a condom to protect his wife from AIDS?

The analogy does not hold. Rain is an agent of life, AIDS of death. A correct analogy would have been laying a tarpaulin on freshly sown ground to prevent it from getting wet.

Paradigm Shifts

A paradigm is a coherent field of thought. The Latin script, used by most languages, is one such paradigm, in the company of 49 others.

Shifting paradigms may be fascinating, funny or downright infuriating depending on the awareness of the shift. The important thing is to recognize it for what it is. The letter H, for instance, is "āch" in English, "ĕn" in Russian and "eta" in Greek. The superimposed X and P, a common Christian symbol, do not stand for the Latin *pax* (peace) but for the Greek chi (ch) and rho (rh) initials of the word XPICTOC (Christ). Similar shifts affect words. **Vita** is "life" in Latin but "war" in Swahili; **salir** means "to get out" in Spanish, "to go up" in Italian and "to soil" in French, etc. Lexicographers call such words "false friends".

Measuring systems offer examples of paradigm shifts that at times do really infuriate users. An engineer I knew was once laying a tennis court with a tape marked in feet. Trusting his measurements, he began calculating, but try as he may he could not get results. He measured and re-measured, but there was nothing doing. Calculations still would not give him results.

In desperation he had an umpteenth look at the tape, and realized the problem: it read **decimal** feet! When he was reading 12 foot five inches, the tape really said 12.5 feet, or 12 foot six inches. His mind and his tape were two different paradigms.

We are so used to reading the symbol 10 as "ten" as not to realize that it can mean any number whatever. We use the ten symbols 0 to 9 in base ten. The numbers one, two... ten are our ten ideas that correspond to ten symbols in that base.

In base two the only two symbols are 1 and 0. One, two... ten are written 1, 10, 11, 100, 101, 110, 111, 1000, 1001, 1010. The rules for the four operations remain unchanged.

Number bases are an excellent example of how "number" is a being of reason, corresponding to a real thing if, and only if, it is an integer in any base.

Different cultures offer many paradigm shifts. During colonial times, a British officer stationed in Somalia was intrigued by a card game, played day after day, by four Somalis squatting in the sleepy square of the town. Try as he might, he could not make sense of it. An equal number of cards were laid out in front of each player. After a while one of them would suddenly rise and collect the stakes.

Defeated, he eventually asked the players what the rules were. The answer bowled him over. The winner was the one on whose cards a fly alighted first! While he was paying attention to combinations and permutations of hearts, diamonds, clubs and spades, the players were vying for the favours of one of Allah's creatures.

Paradigm shifts can also be funny, as the punch line of many jokes is but one of such shifts.

A country parson sees a young country girl leading an enormous bull by the nose.

Parson: Where are you taking that huge beast, dear?

Girl: To serve the cows, Sir.

Parson (slightly uneasy): shouldn't your father do this work, dear?

Girl: O no, Sir, it must be the bull!

Closing this chapter on a light tone, let us continue with what it takes to debate.

CHARACTERS OF CHAPTER TWELVE

SHAW, George Bernard (1856-1950). Play writer, essayist, controversialist and social critic. He combined literary genius (Nobel 1925) with extreme gullibility. He was duped into believing that Communism was paradise on earth following a guided trip to the Soviet Union in the 1930s.

HANNIBAL, 247-192 BC. Carthaginian general, perennial enemy of Rome. Committed suicide after the defeat at Zama.

SCIPIO, Publius Cornelius nicknamed Africanus (237-183 BC). Refused to be named life dictator after the victory over Hannibal, retiring to his farm instead.

DZERZHINSKY, Felix Edmundovich (1877-1926). Head of Lenin's secret police and accomplished mass murderer.

LENIN, nickname of Vladimir Ilyich Ulianov (1870-1924). Inventor of the soviets, councils of workers, soldiers, peasants etc. in control of the entire society on behalf of the communist government. Historians are still trying to figure out how many people died as a result of his policies.

CHAPTER 13

OPPOSITION AND COMPOSITION

Contrary to Sub-Contrary Opposites

If there is no opposition between ideas, there must be coincidence. The expression 4 = 4 is an identity, for the "four" on either side of the equation coincide in symbol and base. Were I to write 4 = 100, 4 = 11, there would be equivalence but not identity, for 100 and 11 are both "four", but in base two and three respectively.

Ideas like "cow" and "circle" are not opposed. Why do they not coincide? Their opposition is metaphysical. "Cow" is a real being with independent existence; "circle" is a being of reason existing only in the mind. Logic cannot solve such problems, hence I leave them out.

Logical opposition between ideas is multiple and varied. Two ideas are **impertinent** when they happen to coincide in or on the same reality, but without relation with one another. That the same person should be learned and portly can happen (St Thomas was like that) but the two ideas remain impertinent.

Other ideas are semi-pertinent. A human is also an animal, but not vice versa: a donkey is an animal but not a human.

Contrary and contradictory ideas have already been explained, but their importance in debating has not. When arguing, it is important that the two positions be contradictory, for only thus must one of the debaters be right and the other wrong. If the opposition is of a weaker kind, say between contraries, both debaters may be wrong.

Parents who argue with their children as to the opportunity of watching television, or playing computer games, may object on the grounds of morals, but not of opinion; to decide that, there is no better way than watching the intended show **together**, so as to judge core contents and not peripherals.

Judgement

The mind composes or separates two ideas by an act of **judgement**. Saying, "Mr So-and-so is a learned man" is a judgement. It implies knowing what man is and what to be learned is. Then it implies grasping that the two concepts "man" and "learned" are pertinent, and finally that they do come together in Mr So-and-so, who is now perceived as a learned man. Denying it by saying, "Mr So-and-so is not a learned man," implies the same grasp except for the last one; the two pertinent ideas are now judged not to coincide in the same person.

The foregoing analyses take place unconsciously. For a student of the process of thinking, however, it is most important to be acquainted with all the individual steps, even without being aware of taking them.

A judgement differs from other operations of the mind in that it is necessarily true or false. It is the most demanding intellectual operation, and that is why it is often difficult to make it.

A judgement contains truth when it affirms what is or denies what is not. It contains falsehood when it affirms what is not, or denies what is. The property of achieving truth or failing to do so is present in **every** judgement and **only** in judgement. All the other operations of the mind: distinction, division and the rest achieve a certain adequacy with things, but the mind is not fully aware of this adequacy until it has made a **judgement**.

CHAPTER 14

COMMUNICATION: TERMS,
PROPOSITIONS AND SYLLOGISMS

When ideas need to be communicated after being worked out within the mind, new problems arise.

The first is that whereas ideas and judgements are non-material, the means of communication: spoken, written or signified, are. We must, therefore, transform ideas into **terms** and judgements into **propositions**. And here there arises a second problem.

A term, whether spoken, written or signified, is an idea in communicable form. But whereas ideas are universal, i.e. common to mankind, terms are not. Each language has its own, and there is no one-to-one correspondence between any two languages, as every translator is only too well aware.

A term is univocal if it stands for only one idea. Such terms offer little difficulty, like "noun," "woman," "dictionary," etc. Univocal terms can be translated from any language to any other without difficulty.

Every language, however, has many terms that are equivocal, i.e. they stand for more than one idea.

Take the English term "stock". It stands for the butt of a firearm, for the source of a family of people or a breed of animals; for raw materials; for a body of knowledge; for a basis for soup, stew, sauce or gravy; for farm animals; for money lent; and for so many more things that to get any further would be too tedious.

Perversely, there exist terms that mean one thing and its opposite **in the same language.** "To cleave" in English means "to split", "to cleave to" means "to stick fast". "To alight" may mean to get out of a vehicle or to get **onto** a surface. Such language idiosyncrasies render thinking harder than it ought to be.

Other terms are **analogical**: their meaning changes with the levels of the hierarchy of being at which they are applied. Take the term "life": one is tempted to apply this term indiscriminately to plants, animals, humans, angels and God. But the term acquires a different meaning at each of the hierarchical levels of being. The different kinds of life are not the same simply because the term is.

The words of every language perform eight or nine functions, but not always in the same way. These functions are found in the so-called **parts of speech**, which in some languages are easily identifiable, in others less so. **Nouns and verbs** form the backbone of a language; pronouns are used instead of nouns to relieve monotony; **adjectives** and **adverbs** modify the meaning of nouns and verbs respectively; and various particles like **conjunctions** and **interjections** lend colour and power to communicated expressions. As functions they exist in all languages, but each language has its peculiar forms to express them. **Prepositions, articles, prefixes, infixes** and **suffixes** appear and disappear from one language to another, at times behaving as terms, at other times not so.

From the viewpoint of this book a **term** is such if it expresses an **idea**, not a grammatical function. It is such terms that a debater must define before embarking in argument. The definition must remain constant, i.e. maintained throughout the debate. This proviso may seem obvious to anyone brought up on the nature of truth as the **correspondence** between mind and reality. It is not at all obvious to people of the Hegelian or Kantian dispensation, some of whom only too easily fall into the habit of admitting the truth of a statement one moment, and contradict it in the course of the same conversation a little later.

The purpose of argument, for such people, is not to reach the truth. Their main preoccupation is values like harmony, face-saving, etc. Their problem is not logical but ethical or sociological, and therefore it does not concern us here.

At times even people who should know the importance of defining a term and maintaining the definition fail to do so. The Heisenberg Uncertainty Principle, for instance, states that the act of measuring a physical interaction actually disturbs the interaction to the extent of making it impossible to **determine** both position and velocity of the interacting particles.

But the term "to determine" conceals a subtle trap. It can mean "to ascertain" or, more dangerously, "to cause". Many scientists argue that Heisenberg destroyed causality with that principle, as he himself did to his dying day. It was Einstein who stood against this interpretation, maintaining that "to determine" means no more than "to ascertain."[21]

Using an equivocal term without telling apart the two meanings is a fallacy of **equivocation**. At the origin stands reduction, the philosophical error that reduces all the aspects of the reality studied to the one best understood, usually measurement. Those who hold this view go so far as to maintain that whatever is not measurable is not real.

Propositions

A **proposition** is the oral, written or signified expression of a judgement. Categorical propositions are of the type "A is B", "A is not B". Hypothetical propositions are of the type "If A, then B;" "unless A, then not B;" "either A or not A, then B;" etc. Hypothetical propositions express what in metaphysics is known as **potency**; categorical ones what is known as **act**.

Propositions can also be classified quantitatively. "All cats are felines;" "all schoolchildren like playing videogames;"

---

21. S. L. Jaki, *Science and Creation*, Scottish Academic Press p. 365.

"all Cretans are liars;" etc., are called **universal affirmative** propositions. Note that being universal and affirmative does not guarantee their truth. As happens here, only the first of the three is true.

The proposition contradictory to the universal affirmative is not, as someone might think, the universal negative, but the particular negative: "some cats are not felines," "some school children do not like videogames," "some Cretans are not liars" are the contradictories.

Contradiction represents maximum opposition. Since the universal affirmatives above are true-false-false, their contradictories are necessarily false-true-true.

The universal negative proposition denies B of all A: "No woman is vain," "no man is green," "no insect is a bird," are universal negative propositions. Their contradictories, all particular affirmative, are "some women are vain," "some men are green," "some insects are birds." Do you get which are true and which false?

In debate it is usually more effective to defend a particular proposition, either affirmative or negative, than to defend a universal one. The reason is obvious: almost every universal proposition admits of exceptions. And remember that exceptions do not prove rules; they destroy them.

Syllogisms

When two propositions have a term in common, it is possible to compare them with one another, **provided the term**

has the same meaning in both. If I say, "all cats are felines; all felines are vertebrates," I can legitimately conclude that "all cats are vertebrates." This kind of reasoning is known as a categorical syllogism, for having two categorical propositions. The propositions being compared are known as **premisses** (sing. premiss) and the third is the **conclusion**.

There is more than meets the eye in the foregoing paragraph. The conclusion is a universal affirmative proposition because the two premisses are also universal affirmatives. Had one of them been particular or negative, the conclusion would also have been particular or negative. This responds to the rule that no more can be said in the conclusion than in the premisses.

The syllogism just proposed has three terms: cat, feline, vertebrate. This responds to another rule, stating that a syllogism must have three, and only three, terms. A syllogism with four terms destroys reasoning as shown below.

The term common to the premisses, "feline", is **univocal**, so that the conclusion is legitimate. Were the term equivocal, no conclusion would be possible. If I say, "No cat has two tails; a cat has one tail more than no cat", I cannot conclude that a cat has three tails. The "no cat" of the first premiss and the "no cat" of the second have wholly different meanings. The syllogism has four terms: no cat (1), two tails, one tail more, no cat (2). The humorous conclusion shows that truth has not been achieved.

I will not bother you with the whole array of rules and regulations that determine whether a syllogism leads to truth or not. Such rules, however, exist, and if you are interested in rigorous reasoning, you should read a proper manual on Logic.

Faulty Syllogisms

In real life faulty syllogisms are more common than one would imagine. With a certain frequency, faulty reasoning is due to sleights of mind that mesmerize the unwary into accepting all sorts of falsehood. Let us consider a few.

Whereas the use of equivocal terms gives away the presence of faulty reasoning, the use of analogical terms is much harder to detect. You may have encountered the following syllogism in some of your school textbooks:

Intelligence is the ability to solve problems; animals do solve problems, therefore animals are intelligent.

The term "intelligence", like the term "life" is analogical. It changes meaning with each step up the hierarchy of being. Therefore there is nothing wrong with this syllogism **as long as its conclusion is confined within the animal level**. Were we to equate animal with human intelligence, the syllogism would have four terms instead of three, two of them taken to be one by the use of words. The term "intelligent" in fact, is as different at the two levels of being as "no cat" was different in the previous syllogism. But equivocation shows the conclusion to be patently absurd; analogy does not. Deciding whether "intelligence" is used univocally or analogically is not a logical, but a metaphysical decision, taken before drafting the syllogism. Which is right and which wrong cannot be done by logic alone. An initial metaphysical error can only beget increasingly worse errors. And, as St Thomas remarks,

He who errs about principle cannot be persuaded.[22]

For clarity, a syllogism cannot have more than three propositions. Adding extra ones leads to dubious conclusions, if any. Consider:

The invention of machinery increased productivity; increased productivity caused the disappearance of slavery; the disappearance of slavery increased the dignity of man. Therefore the invention of machinery increased the dignity of man.

The dubious conclusion is a compound error of faulty reasoning at various levels.

The first is to assume that event a) happening **before** event b) has also **caused** event b). It is the *post hoc ergo propter hoc* (after something therefore on account of something) fallacy.

The second is to accept without proof that increased productivity caused slavery to disappear. Further, the term "slavery" would have to be **carefully defined** to argue that it has

---

22. II IIae Q. 154 12 c

really disappeared. Even ignoring old-time slave markets etc. still thriving in a number of places, the modern world can boast of its own brand of slavery. In 1931 Hilaire Belloc wrote:

> It is in the nature of mankind, when they are proceeding to call that good which once they called evil, to avoid the old evil name… Probably slavery, when it comes, will be called "permanent employment"… [23]

Permanent employment is today avidly sought by many people who prefer security to the uncertainties of entrepreneurship. In the ancient world many voluntarily submitted to old-time slavery because it afforded security, exactly what permanent employment affords today. To equate the two or not would be a legitimate matter for debate, but not here.

The third error is one of confusion between cause and effect. Did the disappearance of slavery increase the dignity of man as the author of the quote maintains, or was rather the acknowledgement of the dignity of man that made anti-slavery legislation possible? The room for argument is vast, so what appears as a four-premiss syllogism is really a chain of reasoning that could profitably be broken into a number of true syllogisms each to be tested separately.

Slogans, clichés and **stereotypes** hardly deserve the name of syllogism. They are conclusions somehow arrived at in the

---

23. *Essays of a Catholic*, Sheed & Ward p. 20.

minds of their proposers, who foist them on the unsuspecting public without revealing how they themselves arrived at them.

Consider this slogan of the birth-control crowd: "A small family is a happy family." No reasoning worth the name ever appears to justify this conclusion, so let us look at experience. This is that where small and large families live side by side, it is invariably the children of small families who go to play in the homes of large families for entertainment. Housework is lighter on the members of large families, shared as it is among many pairs of hands. The elder siblings do not mind looking after the younger ones, thus relieving their parents for more important tasks. It is the principle of subsidiarity at work.

Some famous slogans turned into recipes for mass murder, as Marcus Porcius Cato's "Carthage must be destroyed." 2000 years later, World War I claimed 17 million dead and 20 wounded "to make the world safe for democracy" with not a shred of reasoning behind this shibboleth.

A slogan can be spotted a long way off; a two-proposition syllogism is harder to spot, because it appears reasonable. Consider:

The universe is as orderly as a clock movement, therefore it is a clock movement.

The subtlety of the reasoning lies in the obvious truth of the first proposition. The rub lies with the second (hidden) proposition, which is required by the conclusion. It is "all orderly movements are clock movements". Now it becomes obvious that the argument assumes the two movements **to be at the same level of being**. As this is clearly false, we realize that the argument relies on analogy. It requires proof, which has never been offered.

A common reasoning in biology textbooks concerns spontaneous generation. It goes:

Wherever there is life, there is a certain combination of chemicals; let us therefore assemble those chemicals and we shall get life.

The hidden premiss is

These chemicals, in their postulated order, are a necessary and sufficient cause of life.

This proposition requires proof. But proof is much farther today than it was in Pasteur's time. The electron microscope and molecular biology have uncovered a world of unsuspected complexity behind what was once innocently called "protoplasm", proto-this and proto-that.

You have no doubt heard of the quest for "artificial intelligence" in ever advancing computer technology. The argument is that since computers perform operations at a speed and accuracy undreamed of before, it is a matter of time before they can be made to think for themselves. But, as Stanley L. Jaki remarks,

This is the worst fallacy about computers and artificial intelligence. Machines do not add, they do not calculate, do not integrate any more than a gutter adds and integrates by being the channel for millions of raindrops. In an electronic computer not raindrops but electronic impulses are channelled along strictly pre-determined routes. In the process no addition is performed. It takes a mind, always a mind, to abstract meaning from each step through which the machine is directed by its specific man-built mechanism.[24]

Millions of women have been enticed into working outside the home by the following one-premiss syllogism of the feminist agenda:

Women can do what men do, even better. Therefore let them do it.

The lone premiss is beyond dispute. But there is a second, hidden one, which recites

What men do is more important than what women do.

There is the rub. I have yet to see proof by anyone, man or woman, that driving earth-moving machines, defending criminals, building structures, driving Formula One cars or doing any of the countless things that men do, not out of spirit of dominion but for being attracted by such, is more important than giving birth and educating a unit of human capital.

---

24. *Chance and Reality*, University Press of America.

The world of the media is a fertile ground for misdirected thinking. The irrational drive behind foreign trade is supported by such flimsy reasoning as

The country needs to develop; foreign trade favours development; therefore let us give priority to foreign trade.

The second premiss requires proof. No such proof has **ever** been given, also because "development", defined as "increase in numbers" gets confused with "growth", or increase in size. It can be argued that foreign trade in fact hinders development, but not here.

CHARACTERS OF CHAPTER FOURTEEN

HEISENBERG, Werner (1901-1976). 1932 Nobel Prize for Physics. Philosophically weak like most scientists.

EINSTEIN, Albert (1879-1955). 1921 Nobel Prize for Physics. Whether his theories contributed more to the understanding or misunderstanding of the universe remains to be seen.

BELLOC, Hilaire (1870-1953). Writer of prose and verse, chiefly in English. Acerbic critic of the money power's control of the economy.

CATO, Marcus Porcius, (The Elder, 239-149 BC). Roman statesman and social reformer.

PASTEUR, Louis (1822-1895). Discoverer of microorganisms and promoter of vaccination. Proved wrong by Antoine Béchamp, he accepted defeat on his death bed, but it was too late to undo the damage.

JAKI, Stanley L. (1924-2009). Historian of science and author of philosophical treatises.

CONCLUSION

The contents of this book have been aimed at showing the intimate connection between thinking and the truth of things. But as remarked therein, not everyone sets exclusive store by truth. There are venerable cultures that value other things more than truth. Why should anyone want to give priority to truth?

The answer is that only truth has liberating power, and if you value personal freedom, only truth will deliver it to you. Cultures that value truth are outward looking. Herodotus, the "Father of History", travelled across unknown portions of the world led by curiosity for truth, describing far away people and their customs:

> To prevent the great and wonderful actions of **Greeks and Barbarians** from losing the glory they deserve.[25]

For the Persians of his day, as for virtually all the non-Western people of today, barbarians (people living beyond their borders) deserve no glory. Such inward-looking societies

---

25. Histories 1,1. Emphasis added.

consider themselves as the best, their immediate neighbours next best and so on. There is nothing they can offer to, or take from, barbarians.

It is therefore impossible to conclude this book without reference to the West and its values. Whether the West is to be admired or reviled is open to the reader, but not in ignorance, which should never be an option for an educated person.

The culture commonly called "Western" resulted from the coalescing of three value-systems, conveniently termed the Jerusalem-Athens-Rome axis. They are the Jewish genius for tradition, the Greek passion for truth, and the Roman penchant for justice and for getting things done. If the West is decaying today before our eyes, it is for being no longer loyal to those three value systems.

In this book on thinking I have concentrated on truth as understood by the Greeks. That they valued truth above all else does not mean that they attained it in all fields of human endeavour. They did not know what the human person is, and consequently had no inkling of human dignity. Various forms of discrimination and the institution of slavery were the common features of all ancient peoples.

The liberating power of truth stems from its being taken as correspondence between the mind and things. This correspondence is **ownerless**, as explained earlier. Whether the three values of tradition, truth and praxis came together by accident or by design I will not attempt to state. I wish to point out that it is these values, and not peripherals like race, geography or climate that gave so many Westerners their discoveries in so many fields of endeavour.

Openness to foreign values permitted the West to incorporate Eastern values, such as the symbol 0 for zero, into its culture, with the same zest with which Herodotus incorporated Barbarian lore into his history: for the simple reason that they were **true**.

Another characteristic of truth is that it begets goodness when assimilated and practiced. Athenian truth is the most important of these values. It is not that it "happens" to beget freedom; it is the only thing that begets it. Proof of this is the increasing dependence – not to say slavery – of ordinary people on the powers of the State as well as of their own greed, envy and comfort to name only three. Freedom **from** truth is a contradiction in terms, which has brought nothing but unmitigated serfdom to anyone who has tried it.

The art of thinking, therefore, can only bear fruit if applied on behalf of, and to achieve, the truth of things. I end by wishing readers the same joy experienced by anyone who brings the intellectual powers to bear on the burning questions of the day with method, knowledge, understanding and wisdom. *Bon voyage!*

CHARACTERS OF THE CONCLUSION

HERODOTUS of Halicarnassus (c. 485-425 BC). Travelled widely, collected much material, and wrote the first known set of books in the Western tradition. Cicero dubbed him "The Father of History".

About the Author

Silvano Borruso graduated from the University of Catania, Sicily in 1957 with a doctorate in Agricultural Sciences. He was then appointed assistant lecturer of Systematic Botany at the Botanical Gardens Institute of the university.

Leaving behind what could have been a promising career in academia, in 1960 Borruso volunteered to go to Nairobi, Kenya to be part of the staff of one of the first non-racial school in East Africa. At that time he knew very little English.

Two years later, speaking fluent English, he went on to teach Advanced Level Biology at Strathmore College. The College had very high standards: over 98% of the students qualified for university entrance, some being admitted to leading universities in the world, not a few graduating with first class honours.

Very good company, Silvano Borruso engaged actively in extra-curricular activities: he sang accompanying himself on the guitar, he was an avid and able rock climber who shared his passion with anyone who was interested and was a leading player in the staff vs student soccer matches.

Borruso has authored a number of books on a wide range of topics, readily accessible by browsing on the Internet.